American School Reform

AMERICAN SCHOOL REFORM

Progressive, Equity, and Excellence Movements, 1883–1993

Maurice R. Berube

Westport, Connecticut
London

Library of Congress Cataloging-in-Publication Data

Berube, Maurice R.
    American school reform : progressive, equity, and excellence
movements, 1883–1993 / Maurice R. Berube.
        p. cm.
    Includes bibliographical references and index.
    ISBN 0–275–95036–0 (alk. paper)—ISBN 0–275–95160–X (pbk.: alk. paper)
    1. Educational change—United States—History—19th century.
    2. Educational change—United States—History—20th century.
    3. Progressive education—United States—History—19th century.
    4. Progressive education—United States—History—20th century.
    5. Educational equalization—United States—History—19th century.
    6. Educational equalization—United States—History—20th century.
    I. Title.
    LA217.2.B47   1994
    370'.9'0904—dc20   94–25043

British Library Cataloguing in Publication Data is available.

Library of Congress Catalog Card Number: 94–25043
ISBN: 0–275–95036–0
ISBN: 0–275–95160–X (pbk.)

First published in 1994

Praeger Publishers, 88 Post Road West, Westport, CT 06881
An imprint of Greenwood Publishing Group, Inc.

Printed in the United States of America

The paper used in this book complies with the
Permanent Paper Standard issued by the National
Information Standards Organization (Z39.48–1984).

P

For my grandsons, Nicholas and James Bérubé

CONTENTS

PREFACE

The purpose of this study is to discover common characteristics in American school reform. Finding what variables school reform may possess, I believe, is a valuable task in itself. More important, however, such a study may have public policy implications and serve as a guide to future educational reform.

A major thesis of this study is that there existed in the United States three major school reform movements that were shaped by outside societal forces. Therefore, I have attempted to treat these movements according to the manner by which they were uniquely formed rather than present the movements in toto. Consequently, I have limited the study to public schooling rather than higher education, since education reform has been more concentrated at that level.

I am indebted to a number of people in the preparation of this book. First, I want to publicly thank those reviewers of the manuscript in progress. From Old Dominion University, Dwight Allen, professor of education reform, critiqued the chapters on progressive education and John Dewey; William G. Cunningham, professor of educational leadership, reviewed the chapter on business and education. My son, Michael Bérubé, a professor of English at the University of Illinois at Champaign, contributed useful suggestions on the community control and school culture wars chapters. And my daughter Katherine Bérubé, immersed in feminist scholarship, commented on the Lawrence Kohlberg–Carol Gilligan dispute on moral development.

In addition, the librarians at Old Dominion University and Norfolk State University were especially helpful. The Inter-Library Loan department at Old Dominion was able to secure many important journals not otherwise available. Jack Harton, in the Reference Department, was my personal guide through a maze of computerized information. At Norfolk State, I was privileged to use books from their Black Collection, a repository of civil rights documents.

Bouziane Mohsin helped in translating French professor Sophie Body-Gendrot's book *Ville et Violence*.

Dawn Hall was kind enough to consider this project a priority and diligently typed various editions of the manuscript. My production editor at Praeger, Lynne Feduik Goetz, was extremely helpful in editing the manuscript.

Finally, I have approached the subject with as much scholarly detachment as possible, although I was an active participant in one of the reform movements. But, as the reader will observe, many of the scholars of the respective movements were also reformers.

CHAPTER ONE

THE PROGRESSIVE MOVEMENT

One cannot fully comprehend the great educational reform movements without also considering the societal conditions from which they arose. For, in America, educational reform has been a by-product of larger movements in society. Progressive education, then, was influenced by the progressive movement.

There is a historical consensus of what constituted progressivism. There is less agreement about whether progressivism was a clearly defined movement.

At the heart of progressivism were efforts to expand democracy, sympathy for the immigrant poor, attempts to counterbalance the rise of unbridled wealth with the new industrialism, and a drive against municipal corruption. Specific goals included a fight against big banks and monopolies, regulation of railroads and the food and drug industry, a campaign for child labor laws and women's suffrage, and an emphasis on conservation. Political objectives included direct primaries, referendum and recall mechanisms for political office holders, and a direct election of U.S. senators.

Who were the progressive reformers? By and large, they were comprised of a native-born Protestant middle class who were young and college educated. The birthplace of the progressives was the Midwest. Progressives sought change from *within* American society. On the left, American socialists, comprised of mostly immigrants, sought systemic change *of* the society.

Whether progressivism constituted a coherent movement is under dispute. Progressives came from different segments of the society, and each person or group had a different agenda. Historian Peter G. Filene challenged the view of an organized movement. In an "obituary for the progressive movement," Filene argued that "the concept of a movement seems very much like a mirage."[1] For Filene, unity among progressive leaders was lacking. "Progressivism lacked unity of purpose," he wrote, "either on a programmatic or on a philosophical level."[2] For Filene, the fact that progressives disagreed on goals and strategies was sufficient evidence to convince him of the lack of a coherent movement. A case in point was the issue of prohibition; some progressives favored prohibition whereas others opposed it.

Filene may have overstated his case. Unity in social movements is rarely achieved. The Civil Rights Movement, a half century later, illustrates this point. Black leaders were rarely unified on specific issues. Nonetheless, they agreed on the general goal of lifting the burden of racial oppression. For example, the National Association for the Advancement of Colored People (NAACP) favored legal tactics and eschewed the mass demonstrations of Rev. Martin Luther King, Jr., and the Southern Christian Leadership Council (SCLC). In turn, the Student Nonviolent Coordinating Committee and the Congress of Racial Equality would advance Black Power rather than the goal of racial integration espoused by the NAACP and SCLC.

Closer to the mark was historian Arthur Link's assessment of the progressive movement. "The progressive movement," he wrote, "never really existed as a recognizable organization with common goals and a political machinery . . . [but] . . . progressivism might be defined as the popular effort . . . to insure the survival of democracy in the United States."[3]

THE RISE OF CAPITALISM

The America of the progressive movement was affluent. By 1890, the United States was the dominant industrial economy of the world, achieving what one historian termed as an "astonishing industrial success."[4] And that success brought great wealth, albeit unevenly distributed.

There were a number of reasons for that economic success. The United States was a rich land with abundant natural resources. By 1913, the nation had become the leading producer of coal, iron, petroleum, and electricity.[5] To transport the products from these new resources required a national transportation system. The establishment of transcontinental railroads followed. Moreover, there was a cheap labor supply constantly being replenished by European immigration. American scientists such as Thomas Alva Edison and Alexander Graham Bell made technological advances, such as the electric light and the telephone. Industrialists, such as Henry Ford, contributed managerial breakthroughs such as mass production techniques. Finally, through the assembly lines, the rise of scientific management helped make industry more cost-effective and efficient.

The downside to this economic miracle was cheap immigrant labor. Workers were subjected to long hours and unsafe conditions. Between 1890 and 1907 nearly 18 million European immigrants came to America.[6] The nation's population was by then some 75 million. In 1910, three-fourths of the populations of such urban centers as New York, Boston, Detroit, and Cleveland were either first- or second-generation immigrants.[7] Exploitation of these immigrants, coupled with their European exposure to trade unionism and radicalism, led to a series of bloody strikes and class conflict.

REPRESENTATIVE PROGRESSIVES

Let us examine the life and work of three representative progressive reformers. The journalist Jacob Riis, the social activist Jane Addams, and the theologian Walter Rauschenbusch were prime examples of progressive reformers. One graphically portrayed the darker side of America in his chronicle of poverty, the second was an activist who established a settlement house for the poor, and the third encapsuled the high moral ideal of progressivism in a theology of the Social Gospel.

Jacob Riis

In 1890, Jacob Riis published his account of severe poverty in his classic book *How the Other Half Lives*. Like other progressive reformers of his day, his view of poverty was essentially romantic. That is, he perceived the poor as urban "noble savages" who were victims of society. For Riis and his fellow progressives, poverty did not involve a dark side to the human character. There was little emphasis on crime. In short, the poor were perceived as poor not because of their inner failings of character in a free society, as conservatives believe, but because of a lack of opportunity due to economic constraints and because of ethnic discrimination.

This romantic view resurfaced in the 1960s with the social reformers of the Civil Rights Movement. By 1970, conservatives would counter with the argument that the poor (according to Edward Banfield in *The Unheavenly City*) were poor because of their inability to plan for the future. Whereas romantics emphasized the inherent goodness of the poor, conservatives stressed the negative aspect.

Riis promulgated a romantic vision. "The poorest immigrant," he wrote, "comes here with the purpose and ambition to better himself and given half the chance might be reasonably able to make the most of it."[8] Society, however, was reluctant, according to Riis, to offer that chance. For the poor, Riis argued, "there is no way out" because " 'the system' that was the offspring of public neglect and greed has come to stay."[9] That system would be in large measure responsible for neglect. In the ghettos of New York City, two-thirds of infants would die. The city average was slightly under 50 percent—figures that would be shocking today.[10] Life was cheap. Riis observed that in the summer drowned children would regularly appear "whom no one seems to know about."[11] The poor would abandon children to "foundling homes," and many young men became homeless "street arabs" either to hawk newspapers or begin a life of crime.

Riis viewed the child as the key to social reform. In that respect, he sounded a major theme of both progressive reformers and progressive educators. They viewed poverty through the prism of childhood. Progressive educators would use the term "child" instead of student, constructing an educational philosophy that harked to Jean Jacques Rousseau and the innocence of childhood. "For the corruption of the child," Riis declared, "there is no restitution."[12] He concluded that "the rescue of the children is the key to the problem of city poverty."[13]

Riis did not avoid the issue of crime. However, unlike conservatives, he did not use it as an excuse to ignore the problems of poverty but saw it as responding to liberal governmental action. Riis believed that crime was a result of many causes but "the chief among them . . . the tenement itself."[14] Riis interpreted crime as but "a just punishment upon the community that gave it no other choice."[15]

Riis concluded, rather simplistically, that addressing the problems of housing would solve poverty. His book was subtitled *Studies Among the Tenements of New York*. In New York, fully three-quarters of the population lived in these tenements. The housing was poorly ventilated, had improper sanitation, and was the breeding grounds of starvation and death. Riis concluded that the "security of the other half demands, on sanitary, moral, and economic grounds, that it be decently housed."[16]

Jane Addams

Jane Addams was one of the great progressive reformers. Indeed, "Saint Jane," as she was called in the early 1890s, was chosen as the most popular woman in America in magazine polls before World War I.[17] In her words, she was "considered quite the grandmother of American settlements."[18]

Addams was the founder of the most famous American settlement house: Hull House. Settlement houses were private institutions that helped the poor through a variety of charitable works as well as cultural and artistic endeavours. Hull House became a model for other settlement houses. Its charter declared that the house was "to provide for a center for a higher Civic and social life . . . and to . . . improve the conditions of the industrial districts of Chicago."[19] Hull House provided myriad services: a co-operative to furnish coal and sugar; kindergarten and home arts such as sewing classes; the first public playground in the city; the first coffee house to provide an alternative to the saloon; the first juvenile court; cultural activities such as music and painting classes. In short, Hull House sought a grander vision of possibility for the immigrant poor.

Jane Addams was also a romantic moralist. For her, the poor were initially in a state of grace, only to be brutalized by the crushing weight of poverty. In her reminiscence of Hull House, she wrote:

It was also during this winter that I became permanently impressed with the kindness of the poor to each other; the woman who lives upstairs will willingly share her breakfast with the family below because she knows that they "are hard up"; the man who boarded with them last winter will give a month's rent because he knows the father of the family is out of work; the baker across the street, who is fast being pushed to the wall by his downtown competitors, will send across three loaves of stale bread because he has seen the children looking longingly into his window and suspects they are hungry.[20]

Addams added that "formerly . . . it was believed that poverty was synonymous with vice and laziness," but she claimed that no progressive person would hold these views now.[21]

Three influences shaped her character. First, she adored her father. He was the most prominent citizen in his Illinois county, having been a successful owner of a saw mill, a banker, and a state legislator. Since Jane's mother had died when she was but nine years old, Jane became inordinately attached to her father. Moreover, Jane had curvature of the spine and she considered herself unattractive. Her father made key decisions for her such as the college she was to attend. The death of her father was pivotal. She recalled that for her "a great blow fell."[22] Nevertheless, the trauma rendered her unable years later to discuss the death of her father in her memoirs; she made only a parenthetic reference to his death.

A few years later she was to have a religious experience after seeing a bullfight in Spain. Her enjoyment of the spectacle was to be followed by extreme repulsion. This acute guilt propelled her to devote her life to helping the poor.

Second, she was influenced by Abraham Lincoln. Her father had served with Lincoln in the Illinois legislature and had called him "the greatest man in the world."[23] She considered Lincoln's moral stature to be "the epitome of all that is great and good."[24] She insisted that at Hull House, Lincoln should be held up to the immigrant poor "for their admiration as the greatest American" for freeing the slaves.[25]

Finally, Addams possessed a deep Christian faith. Her search for a vocation had religious overtones. When one examines her life, one is struck by the missionary quality of her work among the poor. Still, her college days at a religious school prompted her to rebel from a fundamentalist religion, then prevalent, and substitute a more universal interpretation of Christianity.

Intellectually, she had much in common with the leading American pragmatic philosophers—William James and John Dewey—whom she knew. For pragmatism, experience was the key. For Jane Addams also, "experience gives the easy and trustworthy impulse toward the right action."[26] Her views on education were colored by the pragmatists' emphasis on experience. She considered the traditional pedagogy outmoded: "We are impatient with the schools which lay all stress on reading and writing suspecting them to rest upon the assumption that the ordinary experience of life is worth little."[27] For Addams, the essence of education in a democratic state was clear. "The democratic ideal," she wrote, "demands of the school that it shall give the child's own experience a social value."[28]

Addams's books consist of a series of homilies intended for a middle-class, college-educated reader. Her major work, *Democracy and Social Ethics*, is comprised of twelve lectures delivered on college campuses. It is not data based but a compilation of insights fashioned into sermons to appeal to a "higher social morality."[29]

Addams was influential in a period of intense social conflict. A number of bloody national labor strikes fueled the growing socialist ranks among workers. Addams was sympathetic to the strikers and not averse to socialism. Indeed, various socialists claimed her as their own. She empathized with those "distinguished Russian revolutionists" who spoke at her Thursday night lectures, seeing them as "belonging to that noble company of martyrs . . . [so] . . . that human progress can be advanced."[30] Nevertheless, her sympathies did not persuade her to renounce her patrician background, and she never joined the Socialist Party.

She did make an important contribution to the emerging feminist movement in America. Addams became a role model for the new college women. She considered herself representative of the New Woman. "Men did not first want to marry women of the new type," she wrote, "and women could not fulfill the two functions of profession and home."[31] In Addams's life, there was virtually no romance, and like a lay missionary she dedicated her life to her settlement work.

In *Democracy and Social Ethics*, she devoted two chapters to the relation of educated women to their families. She hoped to "bring about a healthy compromise" between girls and their parents not accustomed to college-educated women intent on some career.[32] She realized that college for women was a turning point. "Modern education," she wrote of the New Woman, "gives her the training which for many years has been deemed successful for highly developing a man's individuality and freeing his power for independent action."[33]

Addams's popularity ended with World War I. Her opposition to the war made her extremely unpopular. Revisionist historians have criticized Addams and the progressives for their paternalistic demeanor toward the immigrant poor. In *Pluralism and Progressives*, Rivka Shpak Lissak argued that "the myth of Jane Addams does not accord with the realities."[34] The myth was that immigrants were "treated as equals" where "cultures were respected."[35] For Lissak, the reality was that Addams and the progressives were intent on Americanizing the foreign-born poor and stamping out cultural and ethnic values.

Walter Rauschenbusch and the Social Gospel

It was inevitable that the progressive concern for the plight of the poor would find some theological codification. Through the work and writings of Walter Rauschenbusch, a Baptist minister in New York City, this sympathy for the poor was fashioned into a theology termed the Social Gospel. The Social Gospel was to shape the direction of much of American Protestantism for over sixty years. In the 1960s, a survey of Protestant Divinity students revealed that more than half still considered "preaching the social gospel" to be the most notable achievement of American Protestantism.[36]

In essence, the Social Gospel proclaimed that one should direct his or her attention to this world, especially for the plight of poverty, rather than the other world. In his classic statement of the Social Gospel, *Christianity and the Social Crisis*, Rauschenbusch offered an agenda for the churches. The Social Gospel was a "radical new course in Christian teaching and practice" for its day.[37] Rauschenbusch urged fellow Christians to shift focus from the "hope of attaining heaven after death" to reforming "the society in which they lived."[38] He based his argument on a "return to the original, unadulterated teachings of the New Testament."[39]

Rauschenbusch began his ministry in 1886 in New York City. Moved by the poverty of immigrants, he founded an organization a decade later with two other ministers: the Brotherhood of the Kingdom. Along with doing works of mercy, the group published a periodical, *For the Right*, aimed at the working class.

In 1897, Rauschenbusch wrote an article for *The American Journal of Sociology* urging clergymen to become involved in social reform. The article was later expanded to book length in *Christianity and the Social Crisis*, first published in 1907. The book garnered him national acclaim as the major spokesman of the Social Gospel. In this book, Rauschenbusch sought to moor the doctrine of the Social Gospel to the New Testament. First, he chastised the nation with its unbridled capitalism:

Western Civilization is passing through a social revolution unparalleled in history for scope and power. It's [*sic*] coming is inevitable . . . .By universal consent, this social crisis is the overshadowing problem of our generation . . . [but the] social revolution has been slow in reaching our country . . . not because we had solved the problems but because we had not yet confronted them.[40]

Rauschenbusch perceived in poverty not only physical but spiritual degradation, where "the long-continued economic helplessness . . . bears the soul down with a numbing sense of injustice and despair."[41]

In order to solve the "social crisis," Rauschenbusch argued, America must seek not only political equality but economic equality. "We cannot join economic inequality," he contended, "with political equality."[42] Moreover, he wrote, "the sense of equality is the only basis for Christian morality."[43] And he asserted that "social equality can co-exist with the greatest natural differences."[44] In short, inequality due to genetic and environmental differences should also be redressed.

For Rauschenbusch, socialism provided one path. He preached the Social Gospel at the height of the socialist movement in America. Moreover, the Roman Catholic church had issued a series of papal encyclicals that, although condemning Socialism, provided a strategy for liberal social reform. Rauschenbusch concluded that "socialism is the ultimate and logical outcome of the labor movement."[45]

But Rauschenbusch's main purpose was to stimulate the Protestant church to social action. "The church must either condemn the world and seek to change it," he admonished, "or tolerate the world and conform to it."[46] To conform, he warned, would eventually mean the destruction of the church. "If society continues to disintegrate and decay," he prophesied, "the church will be carried with it."[47]

Unfortunately Rauschenbusch's critique lacked a strategy for social reform. He envisioned his task as mainly to alarm a complacent church into social action. He saw social change coming first as personal growth: "The greatest contribution . . . to the social movement was a regenerated personality . . . [with a] will which sets justice above policy and profit."[48]

The Social Gospel was an important link to the moral fervor of the progressive reformers. Historian Arthur A. Ekirch observed that the Social Gospel "supplied the bridge by which Progressivism, as almost a religious faith, and Christianity, as a movement for social reform, were able to join hands and march in unison."[49] Rev. Martin Luther King, Jr., was to be influenced by Rauschenbusch and the Social Gospel.

THE PROGRESSIVE MOVEMENT ASSESSED

Historians have reinterpreted the legacy of progressivism from their own historical vantage points. On one matter they all agree: Progressivism was one of the great movements of social reform in American history. One historian ranks the progressive movement behind the founding of the United States and the Franklin Delano Roosevelt's New Deal that preserved the economic stability of the nation. "The progressives themselves," he concluded, "come in third, an impressive showing."[50]

Progressive historians of the era perceived progressive reform as essentially economic. Basing their arguments on Charles Beard's classic *Economic Interpretation of the United States*, published in 1915, these historians, such as Vernon Parrington, considered the Constitution a "deliberate and well considered protective measure designed by able men who represented the aristocracy and wealth of America; a class instrument directed against democracy."[51] Parrington credited this "discovery of the essentially undemocratic nature of the federal constitution [to be] the chief contribution of the Progressive movement to American political thought."[52]

Beard departed from this progressive critique somewhat. For him, the main problem was not the Constitution but "rather the distribution of wealth and opportunity."[53] Progressive reform meant, then, for these historians economic reform. Some current historians, such as David O. Harris, still feel "that we cannot wholly discount the economic context of progressive reform."[54]

In sum, progressivism meant reform. It was no accident that a major historical analysis of progressivism written by Richard Hofstader in the 1950s was titled *The Age of Reform*. In this book Hofstader perceived the progressive movement as a "status revolution" that corresponded to the political consensus history of his time. By the 1960s, historian stressed confrontation over consensus in the spirit of the Civil Rights Movement. By the 1970s, American historians looked to localized and grass roots history over the broad strokes of the major historical period. Hofstader's *The Age of Reform* is of the classical genre of history on the grand scale with a grand thesis. For him, progressivism was quite simply reduced to status. The status revolution consisted of the Yankee Protestants encountering the immigrant poor whereby "the Yankee found himself outnumbered and overwhelmed."[55] And there were seeds of conflict politically where "the immigrant was usually at odds with the reform aspirations of the American Progressive."[56] But Hofstader interpreted this conflict in status rather than class terms.

Inevitably there would be criticism from the left. Historian Eric Foner, a student of Hofstader's, challenged Hofstader's assessment as not only "dated" but as "elitist."[57] Foner criticized his former mentor for a "deep distrust of mass politics" and a "dismissal of the substantive basis of reform movements."[58]

What is also significant about *The Age of Reform* is that Hofstader failed to mention the role of progressive education despite it being a major contribution of the progressive movement.

There also was a downside to American progressivism. Although progressives laudably sought to help the immigrant poor, much of that aid was paternalistic. Equally important, progressives, especially in the South, continued racist practices. Thomas K. McCraw concluded that on race, "the Progressive contribution was mostly negative and progressive reform exhibited what several historians have called 'a blind spot' toward the problems of race."[59]

CONCLUSION

One historian perceptively viewed progressivism not only "as a broad general movement for reform" but also, significantly, "as an intellectual movement and ideology."[60] Consequently, many of the new progressives had matriculated in Germany for Ph.D.s and invigorated progressive thought.[61] As an ideology, the emphasis was, as a progressive historian wrote at the time, "to strike at poverty, crime and disease; to do everything that government can do to make our country better, nobler, purer, and life more worth living."[62]

In a rising nation with a rising educational class, education was seen as a means toward achieving that "nobler, purer" life. One by-product of the progressives seeking child labor legislation was to have these children receive schooling. It was an age of experts, trained and educated, who would root out political corruption by substituting professionals, such as appointed city managers, for elected mayors and ward bosses who manipulated the immigrant vote.

The concern for the child evidenced in the writings of the progressives spilled over to education. Progressive education was to center itself on the notion of the child, an innocent being to be molded into a citizen fully developing his or her talents.

The great irony, however, is that the progressive concern with poverty would not carry over, wholly, to progressive education. Although some progressive educators, such as Dewey and George Counts, championed social reform, many did not. Rather than developing a pedagogy for the poor, progressive education was designed for the affluent and had its greatest success in elite private schools. In this respect it differed significantly from the Equity Reform Movement of the 1960s. Shaped by the Civil Rights Movement, equity reform of the 1960s stressed the education of the poor through public schools and public monies.

In one respect, the progressives resembled the civil rights leaders of the 1960s. Progressives brought to their movement the high moral tone exhibited by the leaders of the Civil Rights Movement who parenthetically were nearly all religious ministers. In sum, progressivism, like the Civil Rights Movement, was essentially a moral campaign to fulfill the American democratic promise.

NOTES

1. Peter G. Filene, "An Obituary for the 'Progressive Movement,' " *American Quarterly*, Spring 1970, p. 24.
2. *Ibid.*, p. 27.
3. *Ibid.*, p. 31.
4. Sean Dennis Cashman, *America in the Age of the Titans: The Progressive Era and World I* (New York: New York University Press, 1988), p. 20.
5. *Ibid.*, p. 12.
6. *Ibid.*, p. 147.
7. *Ibid.*, p. 109.
8. Jacob A. Riis, *How the Other Half Lives* (New York: Charles Scribner's Sons, 1920), p. 24.
9. *Ibid.*, p. 2.
10. *Ibid.*, p. 15.
11. *Ibid.*, p. 180.
12. *Ibid.*, p. 216.
13. *Ibid.*, p. 185.
14. *Ibid.*, p. 289.
15. *Ibid.*, p. 3.
16. *Ibid.*, p. 282.
17. Rivka Shpak Lissak, *Pluralism and Progressives: Hull House and the New Immigrant 1890–1919* (Chicago: University of Chicago Press, 1989), p. 5.
18. Jane Addams, *Democracy and Social Ethics* (Cambridge, Mass.: Harvard University Press, 1964), p. xli.
19. Jane Addams, *Twenty Years at Hull House* (New York: Macmillan Co., 1945), p. 118.
20. *Ibid.*, pp. 162–163.
21. Addams, *Democracy*, p. 15.
22. *Ibid.*, p. xvi.
23. Addams, *Twenty Years*, p. 23.
24. *Ibid.*, p. 29.
25. *Ibid.*, p. 37.
26. Addams, *Democracy*, p. 5.
27. *Ibid.*, p. 181.
28. *Ibid.*, p. 5.
29. *Ibid.*, p. 180.
30. Addams, *Twenty Years*, p. 402.
31. Addams, *Democracy*, pp. xxxvii–xxxviii.
32. *Ibid.*, p. 75.

33. *Ibid.*, p. 84.

34. Lissak, *Pluralism and Progressives*, p. 182.

35. *Ibid.*, p. 6.

36. Colleen McDannell and Bernhard Lang, *Heaven: A History* (New Haven, Conn.: Yale University Press, 1988), p. 334.

37. *Ibid.*, p. 333.

38. *Ibid.*

39. *Ibid.*

40. Walter Rauschenbusch, *Christianity and the Social Crisis* (New York: The Macmillan Co., 1924), p. 33.

41. *Ibid.*, p. 307.

42. *Ibid.*, p. 251.

43. *Ibid.*, p. 248.

44. *Ibid.*, p. 248.

45. *Ibid.*, p. 408.

46. *Ibid.*, p. 342.

47. *Ibid.*, p. 341.

48. *Ibid.*, p. 351.

49. Arthur A. Ekirch, Jr., *Progressivism in America* (New York: New Viewpoints, 1974), pp. 57–58.

50. Thomas K. McCraw, "The Progressive Legacy," in *The Progressive Era*, edited by Lewis L. Gould (Syracuse, N.Y.: Syracuse University Press, 1979), p. 200.

51. Clyde W. Barrow, "Charles A. Beard's Social Democracy: A Critique of the Populist-Progressive Style in American Political Thought," *Polity*, Winter 1988, p. 253.

52. *Ibid.*, p. 254.

53. *Ibid.*, p. 267.

54. Interview with David O. Harris, professor of History, Old Dominion University, Norfolk, Va., February 4, 1992.

55. Richard Hofstader, *The Age of Reform* (New York: Alfred A. Knopf, 1955), p. 176.

56. *Ibid.*, pp. 180–181.

57. Eric Foner, "The Education of Richard Hofstader," *The Nation*, May 4, 1992, p. 602.

58. *Ibid.*

59. McCraw, "The Progressive Legacy," pp. 191–192.

60. Ekirch, *Progressivism in America*, p. 20.

61. *Ibid.*, pp. 64–65.

62. *Ibid.*, p. 14.

CHAPTER TWO

PROGRESSIVE EDUCATION: THE MATRIX OF IT ALL

Perhaps no educational philosophy so influenced and characterized American education as progressive education. For better or worse, progressive education was shaped by the American society of the late nineteenth century and early twentieth century. In turn, progressive education shaped American education and society through the rest of the twentieth century. It was no accident that its chief philosopher, John Dewey, represented that most American of philosophies—pragmatism.

Progressive education was distinctly American. At a time when the frontier was closing and the romantic myth of rugged individualism was gaining greater currency, progressive education espoused schooling as child centered, where creativity, self-expression, critical thinking, and individualism were to be nurtured. These values have become synonymous with American education and the American character.

If progressive education did not fully realize its potential, it was because of its circumscribed nature. Developed in elite, private schools, progressive education was essentially an educational philosophy for the few, since not many of the poor succeeded educationally, then and now. Progressive education failed to adapt to that growing educational constituency.

That was partly due to a romantic notion of poverty that characterized progressive reformers and progressive educators. With the powerful, nascent capitalism, poverty was sentimentalized. Progressive reformers sought to assimilate the immigrant poor, encouraging them to shed their cultural and ethnic trappings. Moreover, progressive education became the all too willing ally of a corporate state structured on deep-seated inequality. Nevertheless, one must reexamine progressive education in order to understand the dialectic of educational reform in America.

Progressive education was the first and perhaps greatest educational reform movement in the United States. Like the two great educational reform movements that succeeded it—the equity reform movement of the 1960s and the excellence reform movement of the 1980s—progressive education was the offshoot of large societal pressures. In short, progressive education was part and parcel of the larger social movement of the late nineteenth century called progressivism, which sought to reform city and national governments as well as aiding the poor.

What was progressive education? Progressive education was an attempt by educational reformers, psychologists, and philosophers to develop a school experience that would benefit the whole child's intellectual, social, artistic, and moral development. Intellectual development would stress critical thinking, which, defined by John Dewey, essentially meant problem solving.

By contrast, schooling in late-nineteenth-century America consisted of a narrow intellectual exercise. The accent was on rote memorization, which neglected the social, artistic, and moral aspects of learning. Much of the excellence reform movement of the 1980s harks back to the content-driven schooling before progressive education reform.

For progressive educators, the student—the child—was perceived in romantic terms as an innocent whose *whole* personality could be shaped by schooling. The key word was *child*—a softer, more mellifluous word than *student*. It was no accident that progressive education reformers employed the word throughout their works. Book titles proclaimed *The Development of the Child* (Nathan Oppenheim), *The Child-Centered School* (Harold Rugg and Ann Schumacher), *The Child-Centered Curriculum* (John Dewey), and *The Child and the World* (Margaret Naumberg).

For progressive education reformers, the crucial task was to tap the "apparently unlimited desire and interest of children to know and be."[1] The child was to be immersed in a schooling where "he lives in a democracy of youth."[2] A "creative environment" was to be fashioned so that teachers could be "drawing out of the child's inner capacities for self-expression."[3] The buzz-words of progressive education were self-expression, creativity, and individualism. The aim was for schooling that could "develop the child's total personality."[4] For progressive education reformers, progressive education represented "one of the two most important movements in the recent history of education," the other being the campaign for public schools.[5]

Progressive education was on the cutting edge of intellectual progress of its time. It was based on rising scientific discoveries, such as biological evolution and the "new" science of psychology. Progressive educator Margaret Naumberg, founder of New York's Walden School, would proclaim that progressive schools drew on "the most recent findings of biology, psychology and education" so that educators could "discover ways of redirecting and hammering this vital force of childhood in constructive and creative work."[6]

The progressive educators, especially Dewey, were strongly influenced by the eighteenth-century French philosopher Jean Jacques Rousseau. The work that they cited was Rousseau's *Emilé: or an Education,* in which the child was considered an innocent of nature who must be guided through life with an eye to his or her whole personality. (Philosophy professor Allan Bloom, whose own critique of American higher education *The Closing of the American Mind* was to figure prominently in the education reform of the 1980s, was also devoted to Rousseau's *Emilé.* Bloom translated the book in 1979, and it was issued in paperback a decade later. Bloom bemoaned *Emilé's* lack of popularity because contemporary educators had "not held [it] to be of great significance."[7] Bloom hoped that his translation "would contribute to a reconsideration of this most fundamental and necessary book."[8]) For Rousseau nature was paramount. Rousseau proclaimed a philosophy of education that stressed "a natural education."[9] By this he meant that one must direct attention to what the child brings to schooling rather than the reverse. He was explicit on this point: "the closer to his natural condition man has stayed, the smaller the difference between his faculties and his desires and consequently the less removed he is from being happy."[10] Three forces comprise education, according to Rousseau. The first is nature, which is "in no way in our control."[11] The second is the impact of "things," which only occasionally can be controlled. And the last is people, "the only force of which we are truly masters."[12]

Rousseau perceived childhood to be a state of innocence. He was writing at a time when the concept of childhood had only been discovered a century previous. The historian of that concept, Phillipe Ariés, concluded that "there was no place for childhood in the medieval world."[13] Sickness and disease carried off many children so that parents were reluctant to form deep attachments. Consequently, the art of the medieval world pictured children as small adults. With the rise of sanitation and the control of plagues, more attention was paid to the growing child, and formal education became more proscribed.

Against this backdrop, Rousseau commented that "childhood is unknown."[14] Nevertheless, he argued the "incontestable maxim" that nature is "always right" and that there is "no original perversity in the human heart."[15] For Rousseau "nature wants children to be children before being men."[16] Rousseau believed *Emilé* to be his best and most important book.

What Dewey and the other progressive education reformers borrowed from Rousseau was the idea of the child in a state of grace who grows physically, intellectually, and morally. "The very meaning of childhood," Dewey wrote, "is that it is the time of growing, of developing."[17] In short, Dewey credited Rousseau with the concept of schooling as "a progress of natural growth."[18] For Dewey then, Rousseau "sounded the keynote of all modern efforts for educational progress."[19]

Another influence on Dewey (not as great as Rousseau, however) was Maria Montessori. Montessori employed radical educational methods in the first decades of the nineteenth century with retarded and low-income students in Italy. Desks were to be mobile and not bolted to the floor. Students were to learn at their own pace, within a structured environment that downplayed the role of teacher as lecturer.

Dewey was to add to Rousseau's and Montessori's ideas. He fashioned the concept that the best learning was by doing—that ideas were clearest when they could be experienced. This concept was crucial in the pragmatist philosophy he shared with William James. He described progressive schools as those where " 'Learning by doing' is a slogan that might almost be offered as a general descriptive of the way in which many teachers are trying to effect this adjustment [changing the curriculum]."[20]

THE PROGRESSIVE REVOLUTION

With each educational revolution certain tracts became the flashpoints that sparked reform. In 1983 the U.S. Department of Education's study *A Nation at Risk: The Imperative for Educational Reform*, undertaken by the National Commission on Excellence in Education, proclaimed the inadequacies of American education and jumpstarted the excellence reform movement. A century earlier a pediatrician's survey of American schools accomplished the same result in ushering in progressive education reform. Dr. Joseph Mayer Rice's 1892 series of articles on American schools published in *Forum* magazine galvanized public support for school reform. Rice's articles—later published as a book, *The Public-School System of the United States*—shocked the nation.

Rice was a pediatrician who developed an interest in education. He pursued that interest by studying educational methods in Germany for two years, from 1888 to 1890. Returning to the United States, Rice was enthused about the "scientific education" abroad. He publicized these new developments in articles in a small New York City weekly. These articles captured the attention of the editors of the prestigious magazine *Forum*, and they commissioned Rice to assess the state of education in a national study.

During the first six months of 1892, Rice visited major American school systems to observe firsthand the condition of education. He visited thirty-six cities, including the burgeoning urban school systems of New York, Philadelphia, Boston, Baltimore, Chicago, Milwaukee, St. Paul,

Detroit, Cleveland, Cincinnati, and the District of Columbia. Rice observed some twelve hundred teachers and visited twenty teacher training institutions.

He concluded that American education was a disaster. Teaching was "unscientific," geared to the "mechanical" methods of rote memorization and recitation. These schools were not properly administered. Moreover, too few teachers attended "training schools"—the schools of education of the time. Although Rice was primarily concerned with teaching, he also cited the corrupt practices of the day in the appointment of teachers. In too many school systems the hiring practices were subject to the corruption of ward politics.

What Rice meant by scientific methods of teaching was to comprise the essence of progressive education. Citing the insights of the rising science of psychology, Rice proposed a new education that was child centered and emphasized critical thinking. "While the aim of the old education is mainly to give the child a certain amount of information, the aim of the new education is to lead the child to observe, to reason, and to acquire the manual dexterity as well as to memorize facts—in a word, to develop the child naturally in all of his faculties, intellectual, moral, and physical."[21]

It is the "whole child" that Rice argues is the target of the "new" and "truly progressive spirit" of education.[22] The "old system," according to Rice, "forgets the child" whereas "the new system is in large part guided by the fact that the child is a frail and tender, loving and loveable human being."[23]

For Rice, the twin evils of American teaching were that it was "mechanical" and "unscientific." Typical of the conditions in the large urban classrooms were those in New York City where "in no single exercise is a child permitted to think."[24] These schools were those "into which the light of science has not yet entered."[25]

Nor did other big city school systems fare any better. In Baltimore, Rice found "mechanical education almost in its purity."[26] Such schools lacked "any evidence that the science of education had as yet found its way."[27] In Chicago, the one teacher training institute had closed so that Rice found schools in that city in the "highly unscientific class."[28] This condition was repeated throughout his visits to other cities.

But it was Boston that Rice especially targeted. Boston schools were widely regarded as among the best in the nation. Rice would concede that "the schools of no city are in better repute than those in Boston."[29] He would grant that the indices of Boston schools were indeed "ideal," namely, that the spending on education was "extremely high" and that the system was not tainted with political corruption.[30] Nevertheless, for Rice, Boston schools were behind the times. Rice concluded that despite the "superior advantages of the Boston schools," they "fall short of what they ought to be."[31] Boston schools still belonged to the "purely mechanical drudgery schools."[32]

Political corruption was another deficit among the large urban school systems. In Philadelphia, for example, Rice found that teachers were dependent on the political ward systems where "those in authority use their offices for selfish motives, whether political or other."[33] Still, Rice had faith in progressive reform. He termed it the "great educational revolution" that would point American education "in the right direction."[34]

Rice's observations had severe limitations. There were no aggregate data on student achievement by which to measure educational outcomes. Indeed, Rice made no attempt to quantify his study. Rather, his was a journalistic approach that provided highly impressionistic observations of classroom teaching in American schools. Nevertheless, it would be considered a forerunner of qualitative research that employs field notes by a trained observer.

By contrast, the excellence reform movement's study a century later— *A Nation at Risk*—was the opposite. That book relied on quantitative data—much of it challenged by critics—and contained no portrait of what actually happened in the classroom. The reception to Rice's allegations provoked similar public reaction to that of *A Nation at Risk*. The response by the popular press to Rice's study was sympathetic and sent up a strong national alarm system. Nevertheless, Rice was dismissed by the professional press as "merely a sensational critic."[35]

PSYCHOLOGY AND PROGRESSIVE EDUCATION

Progressive education was founded largely on the "new" science of psychology. Perhaps the most influential book to relate the insights of psychology to teaching was William James's *Talks to Teachers*. This book was a compilation of a series of lectures that the philosopher/psychologist made that were extremely popular on national lecture tours.

William James (along with John Dewey) was arguably the most influential American philosopher. The father of pragmatism as a philosophy, James worked both in psychology and philosophy. His writings earned his international recognition. The grandson of a poor, Irish immigrant who went on to amass fortune in colonial America, second only to that of John Jacob Astor, he was heir to both affluence and an intellectual tradition.

James's father, Henry James, Sr., was a disciple of the Swedish philosopher Emmanuel Swedenborg. Henry, Sr., was crippled by a fire that required the amputation of his leg. He devoted the rest of his life to intellectual pursuits. Later, a deep depression resulted, in what his son William was to call a "bundle of truth" that led him to Swedenborg.[36]

William also had his own "bundle of truth" that changed his life. William's younger brother was the acclaimed novelist Henry James. It was said that William was the philosopher who wrote like a novelist and Henry was the novelist who wrote like a philosopher.

Initially, William was interested in painting, but his neurosis propelled him into a study of psychology and philosophy. James was a towering figure in both disciplines. His illness led to his study *The Varieties of Religious Experience*, which stands as a seminal exploration of the psychology of faith. His classic philosophical work was *Pragmatism*, and his major psychological work was *Principles of Psychology*.

James's book *Talks to Teachers* attempted to forge the necessary connection between the discoveries of the "new" science and teaching. His crucial concept was that a child's intellect develops; it is not fixed. He declared that his "main desire has been to make them [teachers] conceive and if possible reproduce sympathetically in their imagination the mental life of the pupil as the sort of active unity which he himself desires it to be."[37]

He charged teachers with a grand purpose. "The renovation of nations begins always at the top," he intoned, "and spreads slowly downward" so that "the teachers of this country ... have its future in its hands."[38] James advocated "a complete professional training" for teachers based on psychological discoveries "to give the teacher radical help."[39] He was confident of the discoveries of the new science of psychology. "Fortunately for you teachers," he told them, "the elements of the mental machine can be clearly apprehended and their workings easily grasped."[40]

His talks were a compendium of helpful hints embedded in an abstract psychological discussion. He told the teachers how to control mental wanderings of pupils, how to improve memory, and how to stimulate a pupil's interest. Moreover, he gently reminded his audience that their task was "to build up character in your pupils."[41] His premise was that the art of teaching had a strong scientific basis. Although his lectures were enormously popular, he would complain that the teachers were "so earnest and so helpless that it takes them half an hour to get from one idea to another."[42]

James viewed the introduction of vocational education—"manual training"—to be the "most colossal improvement in recent years."[43] He also believed that the loose, decentralized system of education in America was "perhaps on the whole the best organization that exists in any country ... [since] the state school systems give a diversity and flexibility."[44]

It is significant that the first major educational reform movement in America would enlist the contributions of the two foremost philosophers in America then and now: William James and John Dewey.

THE PROGRESSIVE EDUCATION ASSOCIATION

The progressive education movement was to acquire a formal organization that would influence American education for nearly forty years. This is especially noteworthy because the other two great educational movements failed to establish key organizations that would funnel the essence of their movements. The equity reform movement of the 1960s had no such organization. The excellence reform movement of the 1980s established an Excellence Network created by Chester Finn, Jr., and Diane Ravitch, educational scholars who had also served in the Department of Education under presidents Ronald Reagan and George Bush, respectively. But the Excellence Network was merely a clearinghouse that had little national presence or a conceptual one.

The Progressive Education Association (PEA) was something altogether different. Founded by educators and concerned parents in 1919 in Washington, D.C., the PEA had as its initial intent "primarily an association of parents and others who are interested in education."[45] It was soon taken over, however, by progressive education reformers from Teachers College, Columbia University. Seven guiding educational principles were initially established. These were "freedom to develop naturally"; "interest—the motive of all work"; "the teacher as a guide not a task-master"; "scientific study of pupil development"; "greater attention to all that affects the child's physical development"; "cooperation between school and home to meet the needs of child-life"; and, finally, "the progressive school: a leader of education movements."[46]

Membership reached a peak of 10,440 in 1938.[47] By contrast, in 1992 the American Educational Research Association had 14,000 members, and the two teacher unions, the National Education Association and the American Federation of Teachers American Federation of Labor–Congress of Industrial Organizations (AFL-CIO), had a combined total of some 2,700,000 members.[48]

Two main developments characterized the PEA. First, the organization was to be dominated in the late 1920s by professors from Teachers College, Columbia University. Teachers College boasted some of the most illustrious progressive educators of the day, including John Dewey, George S. Counts, William Heard Kilpatrick, and the university president Nicholas Murray Butler. Consequently, the PEA mainly reflected the thinking at Teachers College and the leadership of the National Education Association.

Most important, the PEA was never able to clearly define its educational philosophy or agenda. Early emphasis was on individual child development with scant regard for the relationship to society. With the arrival of the Great Depression, the PEA drifted more toward social goals for education, urged in large measure by the provocative work of George

S. Counts. By the 1940s progressive education became diluted to a concept of "life adjustment"; that is, rather than socially reconstruct society, as urged by Counts, education was to prepare (or adjust) a student to the existing social order. Life adjustment became the target of educational conservatives. The idea originated from the Vocational Division of the U.S. Department of Education in the 1940s and was denounced by more socially minded progressive educators such as Dewey.

Symptomatic of the PEA's inability to fix on a clear educational mission was the establishment of a series of commissions that periodically sought to redefine progressive education. Progressive education had an element of vagueness that was to vex the organization. In 1959, the PEA ceased to exist. Nevertheless, it was instrumental in propagating progressive education ideas that held sway for the first half of the twentieth century and have become a distinctive part of American education.

PROGRESSIVE EDUCATION AND THE IMMIGRANTS

In retrospect, perhaps the largest failure of progressive education was in failing to educate the immigrant poor. Conceived in elite, private schools, progressive education was geared for the development of the extremely able child to reach higher plateaus of self-realization. Progressive education portended little for the immigrant poor, who had difficulty in speaking English and whose life chances were severely restricted. Moreover, there was a nativist element in progressive education that sought to Americanize the immigrant by destroying his or her cultural roots.

New York City, the crucible for the waves of immigrant poor that reached our shores between 1880 and 1920, was a case in point. In 1890 43 percent of New York's 1.5 million residents were foreign born.[49] According to one historian, governmental efforts to aid the poor were "minimal."[50] For many nativist Americans, poverty "was thought to be a personal problem."[51] The method of helping the poor was through charity.

The problem of educating the immigrant poor was not met by the school systems. An informative study of the problem in Cleveland, *The School and the Immigrant*, published in 1916 and authored by Herbert Adolphus Miller, a professor of sociology at Oberlin College, graphically presented the indifference of large city school systems. In 1910, Cleveland had the largest percentage—31 percent—(not total numbers) of foreign-speaking inhabitants of any large American city.[52] No less than twenty-nine different languages were spoken by school children, ranging from German to Bohemian. The problem of educating the non-English-speaking poor was formidable.

New immigrants were placed in "steamer classes," so named because they were fresh from the steamships. These immigrants were separated from the mainstream classes as they were considered "misfits in the regular grades."[53] However, they were given "an opportunity to learn the language" before pursuing other studies.[54] They were taught to read in English and not in their native language, as was the case with Hispanics and others in the 1960s in bilingual classes. Miller concluded that the steamer classes in Cleveland met "an important need."[55]

A major problem was mobility. Parents often moved to other neighborhoods without steamer classes, and the children were mainstreamed before they were ready. And in the new schools they were not given any remedial help. Miller observed that "the steamer classes cannot become a very effective instrument . . . until further provisions are made for transporting such children to these special classes."[56] No such aid was forthcoming. Indeed, for the fifteen years prior to Miller's study the Cleveland school administration made no mention of the steamer classes in the annual reports.[57]

Miller ended his brief study on a note of pessimism: "The truth is that the problem of teaching foreign children to speak English has never been regarded by the public schools as one of their serious problems."[58]

Still, progressive educators shared the belief, along with progressive reformers such as Jacob Riis, that poverty could be successful combated. Moreover, they were convinced that "the school was the key to the battle with the slums."[59] This novel idea was to reappear with the equity reformers of the 1960s, only to be challenged by a combination of neoradical and conservative education reformers by the 1980s. Excellence reformers promoted the nihilistic concept that poverty was too large a problem to be solved simply by schooling.

Not that the progressive education reformers did not try. New York City was a critical battleground for the schools to rescue the poor. In 1888, progressive educators formed the Public Education Association that would be a gadfly to school reform to this day. The first head of the PEA was a twenty-seven-year-old school reformer and Columbia University professor Nicholas Murray Butler. One historian dubbed Butler "the Field Marshall of the school reform movement."[60] Butler founded the teacher training institute that was to become Teachers College at Columbia, a hotbed of progressive education reform. Later he was to distinguish himself as president of Columbia.

For Butler, New York schools failed to reflect the new ideas of progressive education. In concert with other city reformers, he wished to see the outdated curriculum and teaching methods conform with new ideas of child development. Moreover, as the "leading spokesman for school reform" he urged centralization of the New York City school system and renovation of school buildings.

Some of the progressives' ideas to combat the nefarious influence of the slums have been recycled. Progressive reformers recommended a longer school day and a longer school week—proposals that would resurface a century later with the excellence reformers but with a different constituency in mind: grooming the best and the brightest to revive a sagging American economy.[61]

Primitive capitalism in the late nineteenth century featured many unskilled jobs. In 1900, 90 percent of the jobs required little skill and little education: a century later 90 percent required greater skills and increasing levels of education, and only 10 percent were unskilled.[62] Consequently, progressive educators were confronted with a huge dropout rate for students who joined the workforce mainly to help their families. In 1914, 50 percent of New York City students left elementary school at age fourteen to work—the age when one could obtain working papers.[63] In high school, 30 percent more dropped out.[64] A century later the New York City dropout rate in high schools with a new black and Hispanic poor was 29.4 percent (1988) with another 25 percent retained for a fifth, sixth, and seventh year of high school.[65]

Progressive education did not sufficiently adapt its methodologies and insights to have a beneficial effect on the children of the poor. Progressive education began in private schools, and although it eventually encompassed public schools it was an ideology best suited for children of the affluent. Self-expression, creativity, and child-centered activities represent a stage of intellectual development that is best taken advantage of by students who have no concern about cramped sleeping quarters or hunger. In short, progressive education, despite its noble aims, was ill suited for the immigrant poor.

Popular and scholarly misconception had long held otherwise. Leo Rosten's nostalgic 1930s novel *The Education of Hyman Kaplan* glorified the success of immigrants in school. Moreover, as late as the 1970s ethnic sociologist Rev. Andrew Greeley would hail the "ethnic miracle."[66] The facts were otherwise. In a seminal 1972 study, *The Great School Legend*, revisionist historian Colin Greer demolished the myth of success in the schooling of immigrants. Greer observed that "from 1890 on . . . in virtually every study undertaken . . . more children have failed in school than succeeded."[67] Greer examined in detail the school systems of five major cities and a number of smaller cities during the period 1880–1920 during the great European migrations. The larger cities included New York, Chicago, Philadelphia, and Boston. Greer found that no more than 60 percent of students were at grade level in these school systems. He would conclude that the failure to reach the immigrant poor in urban classrooms was due to "the essential conservatism of American reform movements."[68]

Another issue was acculturation. Nativist Americans were fearful of the new immigrants, despite the economy's reliance on them for cheap labor. Consequently, efforts were underway to reshape the immigrant into a homogenized American. Typical of these sentiments was the enormously popular 1908 play on assimilation written by a British Jew, Israel Zangwill, entitled *The Melting Pot*. Nevertheless the melting pot was somewhat difficult to achieve. In New York City, of the 1 million Jews, 250,000 of them were reading the Yiddish newspaper *The Jewish Daily Forward*.[69] The Roman Catholic church became "the principal church of immigrants" with 10,000 parishes in 1900, many of them foreign language.[70]

The Great Immigration from Europe resulted in a native backlash. In 1924, federal immigration laws "virtually closed the nation's doors" to Europe.[71] There was an inevitable hostile reaction of nativist Americans to the new immigrant society. Even President Theodore Roosevelt preached the values of nativism.

The public school became an arena to Americanize the immigrants. It was to be "the center of assimilation" where any trace of foreign culture was to be eliminated.[72] Consequently in 1884 Catholic schools were created to escape nativist prejudices, and within six years some 600,000 students were in parochial schools.

Students in the public schools were to learn to read and write in English. There were no attempts at a bilingual approach to soften the difficult transition from one language to another. The American virtues of cleanliness, hard work, thrift, individualism, and patriotism became hallmarks of the American public school. A half century later, revisionist historian Michael Katz criticized "the racist implication" of the nativist approach:

It was, after all, implicit in the "common" of the "common school" that education should forge social unity by blurring cultural distinctiveness—the familiar idea of the melting pot.

What is less obvious, although closely related, is the racist implication of such a point of view. If an attitude that considers one group to be different from and inferior to another in some basic and essential fashion can be labelled racist, then we are forced to the conclusion that racist sentiment scarred the origins of public education . . . . In the course of a century, the particular object has changed from Irish Catholic to black but the attitude remains.[73]

PROGRESSIVE EDUCATION AND THE SOCIAL GOSPEL

There were attempts by some progressive reformers to go beyond the focus on individualism of progressive education. The Social Gospel movement of the turn of the century influenced some progressive educators. One historian concludes that "the social gospel movement supported the Progressive education movement."[74] A case in point was

John Dewey. Raised in an evangelical Protestant family, he drifted away from Christianity and simply substituted the secular Social Gospel for his religious background.

At the heart of progressive education was a strong moral impulse. There was an assumption to progressive education that embodied, according to the literary critic Malcolm Cowley, "the idea of salvation by the child."[75] Cowley was more explicit: "If a new educational system can be introduced, one by which the children are encouraged to develop their own personalities to blossom freely like flowers, then the world will be saved by this new generation."[76]

There were more concrete calls to save the social order. Teachers College professor George S. Counts would challenge his fellow progressive educators to turn from the individualistic content of their educational programs to a more socially conscious orientation. In 1932, at the height of the Great Depression, Counts delivered a stinging and controversial address at the Progressive Education Association convention. Published as a fifty-six-page pamphlet entitled *Dare the Schools Build a New Social Order?* Counts's message was simple and direct. He urged his fellow reformers to instill in the new generation of students social consciences so that they may one day redress the inequities of an unjust society. There were no appeals for the schools to organize social reformers or for the PEA to act as a political pressure group. The political development of educators would not occur until some thirty years later when the two teacher unions (NEA and AFT) would enter political campaigns supporting specific politicians.

Counts's critique was essentially a negative one. He berated his fellow reformers. Although he would credit progressive education with "a number of larger achievements" he felt that it was "not enough."[77] Rather he informed his colleagues that "the weakness of Progressive education . . . lies in the fact that it has elaborated no theory of social welfare."[78] Instead, they had promoted the status quo. American schools, he charged, "instead of directing the course of change are themselves driven by the very forces that are transforming the rest of the social order."[79] Yet, education for Counts was "the one unfailing remedy for every ill to which man is subject."[80] This unqualified faith in the powers of education to solve all problems would resurface in the 1960s with the equity reform movement; it would be espoused by such as President Lyndon B. Johnson.

Counts offered few concrete proposals to build a new social order. At best, he urged that teachers "deliberately reach for power and make the most of the conquest."[81] Still, in depression America, Counts helped redirect the debate among progressive education reformers.

CONCLUSION

How successful was progressive education? The historical consensus from all vantage points—left, right, and center—is that progressive education left an indelible imprint on American education. For centrists, such as the historian Lawrence Cremin, progressive education beneficially shaped American education for the next century. For Diane Ravitch, a neoconservative critic, "progressive ideas had transformed the American public school during the first half of the twentieth century."[82] For the leftist revisionist historians, it was not what progressive education accomplished so much as what it did not accomplish.

Perhaps the most positive appraisal came from Teachers College professor Lawrence Cremin, major historian of progressive education with his 1962 study *The Transformation of the American School*. Cremin chronicled an admiring portrait of progressive education. "The progressive vision," he wrote in 1961, "remained strongly pertinent to the problem of mid-century America."[83] Not surprisingly, Cremin was working on a biography of John Dewey at the time of his death in 1990.

Perhaps the most negative appraisal came from the conservative right. Critics in the 1940s and 1950s charged progressive education with no less than subversion of American education. They felt that rigorous academic work in the basic subjects was replaced by less rigorous courses. A chief and persistent critic in the 1950s was Admiral Hyman G. Rickover, credited with developing the atomic submarine. In a series of speeches, later published in 1959 as *Education and Freedom*, Rickover typified the criticism of progressive education from the right. Rickover argued that progressive schools, by emphasizing life adjustment, were not as rigorous in teaching core subjects "such as algebra, French, or physics."[84] He contended that America could no longer afford for "education [to] be left to the 'professional educators.' "[85]

By the 1950s, the conservative attack on progressive education succeeded. Progressive schools were ridiculed in the popular media. A highly successful Broadway play and film, *Auntie Mame*, about a Greenwich Village eccentric, was one example of the ridicule aimed at progressive education.

By the 1980s the reformers of the excellence movement could find no common ground with progressive education. With the espousal of core subjects and stress on basic subjects, excellence reformers, such as Diane Ravitch, could critique progressive education for what they perceived as a *rejection* of "the belief that the primary purpose of the school was to improve intellectual functioning."[86]

Other criticism came from the revisionist historians of the late 1960s and early 1970s. So called because they attempted to "revise" myths of public schooling, these historians reflected the social consciousness of the

1960s. Their work reflected new advances in historical methodology, examining quantitative records such as school board votes and test scores in localized settings. The originality and strength of their evidence made them the dominant educational school for over a generation.

The revisionists scored the progressive education movement on a number of counts. First, they argued that progressive education was a mere appendage of a raw capitalistic system that preferred a reserve army of unemployed for structural transitions. Second, they accused progressive education of fostering nativism, thus damaging ethnic heritage and culture. Third, they perceived progressive education to be but another attempt to restrict social mobility and keep the poor in their place.

One example illustrates the severity of the revisionist attack. In his monograph *Education and the Rise of the Corporate State*, published in 1972, Joel Spring accused the progressives of promoting "education for social control."[87] Spring concluded that the American public school "is and has been an instrument of social, economic, and political control."[88] American business perceived in the promotion of vocational education by progressives an opportunity for a skilled workforce. Moreover, the emphasis of progressive education on social interaction—adjustment to society—coincided with the search for docility and organization men in corporate bodies.

Progressive education passed away largely because it no longer was relevant. Progressivism died, Diane Ravitch observed, "largely of old age."[89] Equity reformers in the 1960s asked new questions about educating the poor, for which progressive education had no answers. For the excellence reformers of the 1980s, the threat of economic competition and poor performance in the schools demanded an approach that was rigorous and dealt with basic academic subjects. In short, progressive education was no longer progressive.

Nevertheless, progressive education was to define the vision and content of an educational system that was distinctly American. A more fitting obituary would be the assessment of a former director of the Progressive Education Association. Frederick L. Rederfer concluded that progressive education was "the most important educational movement [of its time] . . . [whose] contributions were absorbed in one form or another by all schools and institutions and can still be seen throughout America in full flower or diluted form."[90]

NOTES

1. As quoted in Lawrence A. Cremin, *The Transformation of the School: Progressivism in American Education 1876–1957* (New York: Vintage, 1961), p. 211.

2. Harold Rugg and Ann Schumaker, *The Child-Centered School* (Yonkers, N.Y.: World Book Co., 1928), p. 2.

3. *Ibid.*, p. 8.
4. *Ibid.*, p. 9.
5. *Ibid.*, p. iii.
6. Cremin, *The Transformation*, pp. 211–212.
7. Jean Jacques Rousseau, *Emilé: or an Education* (New York: Basic Books, 1979), p. vii.
8. *Ibid.*
9. *Ibid.*, p. 84.
10. *Ibid.*, p. 81.
11. *Ibid.*, p. 38.
12. *Ibid.*
13. Phillipe Ariés, *Centuries of Childhood* (New York: Vintage Books, 1962), p. 33.
14. Rousseau, *Emilé*, p. 92.
15. *Ibid.*
16. *Ibid.*, p. 90.
17. John Dewey and Evelyn Dewey, *Schools of To-Morrow* (New York: E. P. Dutton, 1915), p. 6.
18. *Ibid.*, p. 17.
19. *Ibid.*, pp. 1–2.
20. *Ibid.*, pp. 70–71.
21. Joseph Mayer Rice, *The Public-School System of the United States* (New York: Arno Press, 1969), p. 21.
22. *Ibid.*
23. *Ibid.*, pp. 22–23.
24. *Ibid.*, p. 38.
25. *Ibid.*, pp. 30–31.
26. *Ibid.*, p. 55.
27. *Ibid.*, p. 61.
28. *Ibid.*, p. 169.
29. *Ibid.*, p. 121.
30. *Ibid.*
31. *Ibid.*, p. 123.
32. *Ibid.*
33. *Ibid.*, p. 147.
34. *Ibid.*, p. 230.
35. Cremin, *The Transformation*, p. 6.
36. Gay Wilson Allen, *William James: A Biography* (New York: Viking Press, 1967), p. 18.
37. *Ibid.*, p. 384.
38. William James, *Talks to Teachers* (New York: Henry Holt and Co., 1925), p. 3.
39. *Ibid.*, p. 5.
40. *Ibid.*, p. 11.
41. *Ibid.*, p. 184.
42. Allen, *William James*, p. 389.
43. James, *Talks to Teachers*, p. 35.
44. *Ibid.*, p. 230.

45. Cremin, *The Transformation*, p. 245.

46. *Ibid.*, pp. 243–245.

47. *Ibid.*, p. 257.

48. Maurice R. Berube, *Teacher Politics: The Influence of Unions* (Westport, Conn.: Greenwood Press, 1988), p. 3.

49. Diane Ravitch, *The Great School Wars* (New York: Basic Books, 1974), p. 108.

50. *Ibid.*, p. 107.

51. *Ibid.*

52. Herbert Adolphus Miller, *The School and the Immigrant* (Philadelphia: Wm. F. Fell Co., 1916), p. 17.

53. *Ibid.*, p. 73.

54. *Ibid.*

55. *Ibid.*

56. *Ibid.*

57. *Ibid.*

58. *Ibid.*, p. 75.

59. Ravitch, *The Great School Wars*, p. 111.

60. *Ibid.*, p. 144.

61. *Ibid.*, p. 191.

62. U.S. Department of Commerce, *Population Profile of the United States 1993* (Washington, D.C.: U.S. Government Printing Office, 1993), p. 25.

63. *Ibid.*, p. 190.

64. *Ibid.*

65. Interview with Noreen Connell, executive director, Educational Priorities Panel, New York City, January 5, 1994 (telephone).

66. Andrew Greeley, "The Ethnic Miracle," *The Public Interest*, Fall 1976, pp. 20–36.

67. Colin Greer, *The Great School Legend* (New York: Basic Books, 1972), p. 108.

68. *Ibid.*, p. 60.

69. Ravitch, *The Great School Wars*, p. 176.

70. *Ibid.*

71. *Ibid.*, p. 174.

72. Ravitch, *The Great School Wars*, p. 185.

73. Michael Katz, *Class, Bureaucracy and the Schools: The Illusion of Educational Change in America* (New York: Praeger, 1971), pp. 39–40.

74. Takahisa Ichimura, "The Protestant Assumption in Progressive Educational Thought," *Teachers College Record*, Spring 1984, p. 451.

75. *Ibid.*, p. 453.

76. *Ibid.*, p. 454.

77. George S. Counts, *Dare the School Build a New Social Order?* (New York: Arno Press, 1969), p. 5.

78. *Ibid.*, p. 7.

79. *Ibid.*, p. 3.

80. *Ibid.*, p. 3.

81. *Ibid.*, p. 28.

82. Diane Ravitch, *The Troubled Crusade: American Education 1945–1980* (New York: Basic Books, 1983), p. 45.

83. Cremin, *The Transformation*, p. 353.

84. Hyman G. Rickover, *Education and Freedom* (New York: E. P. Dutton, 1959), p. 136.

85. *Ibid.*

86. Ravitch, *The Troubled Crusade*, p. 44.

87. Joel Spring, *Education and the Rise of the Corporate State* (Boston: Beacon Press, 1972), p. 162.

88. *Ibid.*

89. Ravitch, *The Troubled Crusade*, p. 78.

90. Frederick L. Rederfer, "What Has Happened to Progressive Education?" *The Education Digest*, September 1948, p. 52.

CHAPTER THREE

JOHN DEWEY: AMERICA'S EDUCATIONAL PHILOSOPHER

John Dewey was one of America's great philosophers. He considered himself "first, last, and all the time, engaged in the vocation of philosophy."[1] Dewey was also the great philosopher of education whose ideas gave American education its unique character. Dewey's influence has lasted for nearly a century. He has become identified with American education. But no thinker with such a lasting influence can escape revisionism. By the mid-twentieth century Dewey came under attack from the left and right. Nevertheless, one cannot comprehend education in the United States without understanding John Dewey.

DEWEY'S LIFE

There were three dimensions to John Dewey's life. First, he was a philosopher; second, he was an educator; and third, he was a social activist. His was an extremely active life. Dewey wrote 40 books and some 700 articles, but he found the time and energy to devote himself to educational, political, and social causes. Dewey was the precursor to the "engaged intellectual" of the modern and postmodern eras in the United States and Europe.

After philosophy, education was his second love. As the United States' preeminent educational philosopher, he was a school teacher, a principal, and a college professor. Also, he directed an experimental laboratory school. Dewey's educational philosophy was an outgrowth of his philosophical ideas of pragmatism or his version of that distinct American philosophy, instrumentalism. Dewey's educational philosophy was to constitute the core of progressive education. He remains the most significant thinker in American education.

Dewey's life was long. A New England Yankee reared in the tradition of hard work, Dewey was born in Vermont in 1861 and died in 1952. His parents were not especially education minded. His father was a grocer. But both parents enjoyed reading, and Dewey's mother encouraged him to attend college. They were evangelical Protestants and were rather liberal for their time on religious issues.

At the age of 16, Dewey entered the University of Vermont. This was before mass higher education; the entire student body was comprised of but ninety-four students with eight faculty. He graduated two years later at the age of 18, second in his class and Phi Beta Kappa.[2] Dewey's main college academic interests were political and social philosophy.

John Dewey's lifelong interest in education came early. After graduating from the University of Vermont, he both secured a teaching position and served as an assistant principal in a public high school in Oil City, Pennsylvania. The faculty consisted of but three members, the other two being women.[3] He stayed two years and returned to Vermont to teach at a private school with some thirty-five students. After two years at the Charlotte school in Vermont, he decided to pursue a doctorate at Johns Hopkins University.

Ironically, the father of progressive education was not an especially effective teacher in high school nor a captivating professor later in college. He was liked but also was a source of ridicule. He lacked the stern qualities of a disciplinarian in high school. His college teaching was no better, but his problems were of a different nature. Even his biographer concedes that Dewey "seemed to lack all the essentials of a good teacher."[4] He delivered his lectures seated, speaking in a slow drawl and gazing out the window. His students considered his classes a "boring experience."[5] Indeed, students at the University of Chicago had compiled a "sophsters New Dictionary" with the following definition: "Dew(e)y.—Adj. Cold, impersonal, psychological, sphinxlike, anomalous and petrifying to flunkers."[6]

Despite his lackluster teaching style, Dewey's academic career was distinguished. He taught at prestigious universities such as Michigan, Chicago, and Columbia. He retired from college teaching in 1930, but he continued his writing and involvement until his death a generation later.

Nor was Dewey's writing style any more dynamic. His writing consisted of grand ideas embedded in the most pedestrian prose. It proves a challenge to readers, especially the postmodern ones. Even his most sympathetic contemporaries despaired of Dewey's proletarian prose. Supreme Court Justice Oliver Wendell Holmes characterized Dewey's books as "what God would have spoken had he been inarticulate."[7]

Beyond public school, college teaching, and his writing, Dewey's involvement in education was extensive. At the University of Michigan, he founded a Schoolmasters Club, which brought college professors and school personnel in contact—a precursor to the Principals' Centers originated by Harvard professor Roland Barthes in the 1980s. At Chicago, he was instrumental in the formation of a separate Department of Education—an uncommon feature in universities at the time. In addition, he created a Pedagogical Museum that displayed the latest educational textbooks and reference works. He introduced round table discussions for school teachers on current educational issues.

Most important, he created a laboratory school. A pioneer venture, the laboratory school was to serve as a place to experiment with new educational methods and curricula. The school at Chicago lasted but six and a half years, yet it served as a model for other university laboratory schools, some of which exist to this day. The Chicago school grew from 16 students to 140 students with 23 teachers in its last year.[8] After the first director resigned because of health, Dewey assumed the directorship of the school. Along with his daughter, Evelyn, Dewey reported on that experience in his book *Schools of To-Morrow*.

At Columbia, Dewey had a joint appointment in the departments of philosophy and education. In the latter, he taught an occasional course and was involved in that university lab school—the Horace Mann Schools for Boys and Girls.

Moreover, Dewey was extremely active in teacher organizations. Dewey was a member of the American Association of Universities, the National Education Association (NEA) and the American Federation of Teachers (AFT). He was a founding member of the AFT and urged it to affiliate with the organized labor movement, the American Federation of Labor. Dewey strongly argued for teachers to join these organizations. In a 1916 meeting of the AFT, he outlined his reasons why teachers should do so:

We have lacked a sense of loyalty to our calling and to one another, and on that account have not accepted to the full our responsibilities as citizens of the community.

To my mind, that is the great reason for forming organizations of this kind . . . which are affiliated with other working organizations . . . like the Federation of Labor.[9]

Dewey perceived merit in both the NEA and the AFT, the former with its professional bent and the latter with its union perspective. He hoped that these organizations could join "the education interests which are discussed in a purely theoretical way, and those other more practical concerns."[10]

Dewey was a social activist. In the words of one sympathetic critic,

Dewey was on "the advanced edge of social change."[11] Dewey's views and involvement in politics and social change can best be described as liberal reformist. It was no accident that many of his articles on politics and social change were published in the intellectual journal *The New Republic*. Under the editorship of Herbert Croly, *The New Republic* became the beacon for liberal reform, which, purportedly, would rescue the "American promise" (the title of Croly's major opus) from America itself. And Dewey became one of America's chief liberal spokespersons.

Some present-day critics label Dewey a "democratic socialist."[12] This says more about current democratic socialism than about Dewey. Although Dewey was sympathetic to American socialism of the early twentieth century, he never became a member of the Socialist Party. Dewey's social philosophy was more liberal reformist, as is much of current democratic socialism. In Dewey's era, socialism presented a viable alternative. In 1912, Socialist Party leader Eugene Debs amassed 897,000 votes, almost 6 percent of the popular vote.[13] Today, Democratic Socialists constitute an esoterically small group situated mostly in the universities and trade unions.

Dewey took strong positions on major sociopolitical issues. He founded an independent party in the 1920s that took positions somewhere between the socialists and the mainline parties. He was active in the newly formed American Civil Liberties Union. He helped found the New School for Social Research. Dewey was instrumental in the expulsion of the Communist-dominated locals of the American Federation of Teachers in the 1930s. He argued for the release of Sacco and Vanzetti, two anarchists executed for alleged murder in a Massachusetts robbery. Most important, he was a key member of an American commission that exonerated Leon Trotsky from charges of treason in the 1936 Moscow Trials in the Soviet Union.

One must keep in mind that Dewey was writing about education reform at a time when both public and higher education were not mass enterprises. When Dewey first came to Columbia University to teach, the student body numbered 4,981. When he retired in 1930, that number grew to over 38,000.[14] By 1993, enrollment dropped to 19,800.[15] Moreover, Dewey was involved in political and social issues during a time of turbulent social unrest both nationally and internationally.

DEWEY'S PHILOSOPHY OF EDUCATION

Let us consider three main works in the Dewey canon. *Democracy and Education, The School and Society,* and *Schools of To-Morrow* reflect different aspects of Dewey's thinking. In one, Dewey viewed education through the democratic political prism; in another, he studied the societal infrastructure of learning; and in another he fleshed out theories of progressive education as practiced in a laboratory school.

Democracy and Education is Dewey's major work. This classic text summarizes Dewey's main educational ideas. The main thesis of *Democracy and Education* is how progressive educational ideas best fit a democratic political system. This work clearly presents Dewey as a major philosophical apostle for liberal democracy.

Scholars have noted Dewey's philosophy to be concerned with a dualistic matrix. Dewey perceived his philosophical task to reconcile the dualism he saw in mind and matter. *Democracy and Education* is full of such dualisms. Besides the two main ideas that form the title of the book, Dewey discussed the relationships of the "individual and the world," "intellectual and practical studies," "inner and outer" modes of learning, "intelligence and character," and "the social and the moral."

Dewey announced his aim in the book to be "no less than to apply the ideas in a democratic society" to "the problem of the enterprise of education."[16] For Dewey, there could be no real learning without the political freedom implicit in a democratic society. In Dewey's words, "lack of the free and equitable intercourse of [ideas] makes intellectual stimulation unbalanced."[17] Education, he argued, is a "social process" that implies "a *particular* social ideal."[18] Dewey concluded that in terms of education "the devotion to democracy is a familiar fact."[19]

Dewey's vision of democracy was a liberal one, devoted to pursuing a social ideal. He wrote of "education as a social function" whereby teaching, essentially, consists of "social direction."[20] The classroom constitutes for Dewey a "social environment."[21]

Despite present-day allegations that he did not stress intellectual rigor, Dewey make clear in *Democracy and Education* that the main aim of education is to develop intellectual abilities. For Dewey, that consists of equating thinking with problem solving. "If he [the student] cannot devise his own solutions," Dewey wrote, "and find his way out, he will not learn."[22] In short, "ideas have to have their worth tested experimentally."[23] This is the essence of pragmatism.

Such an axiom changes the nature of teaching. What is proposed is "a classroom social environment" whereby "learning is achieved through doing."[24] Dewey condemned the lecture method as meaningless. "No thought, no idea," he wrote, "can possibly be conveyed from one person to another."[25]

Moreover, in *Democracy and Education*, Dewey showed that he was also concerned with content. "History and geography," he declared, "are the information studies *par excellence* of the schools."[26] And science is no less than "the agency of progress in action."[27]

In addition, Dewey was concerned with moral education. He conceded that "the establishing of character is a comprehensive aim of school instruction."[28] But he quickly added that moral education is "practically hopeless" when "the development of character" is proposed as the "supreme end" and "at the same time . . . the acquiring of knowledge . . . [is treated] as having nothing to do with character."[29] Nevertheless, Dewey argued for both "play and work in the curriculum," which has often led both critics and followers to perceive Dewey as placing less stress on intellectual rigor.[30]

Dewey's attempt to reconcile democracy and education has serious drawbacks. The proposition that true learning is only a staple of a democratic political system is simplistic. Despite the handicap of orthodoxy, some closed systems have, nevertheless, been able to achieve certain intellectual accomplishments. The Middle Ages produced a richness in art, and the Communist societies achievement in science.

Moreover, Dewey is not sufficiently critical of liberal democracy. Racism and sexism have been concomitant products of that society. Research indicates that low teacher expectations deter the progress of poor African Americans. Studies also show that teachers favor males over females in teaching. As American history indicates, democracy is a flawed political instrument that has to be corrected for disparities of wealth and for racist and sexist biases.

But Dewey had a strong social vision. In *The School and Society*, published in 1900, he attempted to link the "new education" with the need to reconstruct capitalist society. *The School and Society* is the first major attempt to employ education as a saving remnant for American society. The book consists of three lectures on the relationship of education to social change, plus a listing of the guiding principles for Dewey's laboratory school at the University of Chicago.

Dewey was clear on the need for the "new education" to be fashioned "in the light of larger changes in the society."[31] The societal change that for Dewey "overshadows" all others—"industrialization—requires a schooling appropriate to the demands of a new century."[32] Dewey argued that "it is radical conditions which have changed, and only an equally radical change in education suffices."[33] And that radical educational change must have a social base. For the "new movement in education," Dewey intoned, "it is especially necessary to take the broader, or social view."[34]

Dewey favored the nurture side of the debate on intelligence. He perceived intelligence not mainly to be hereditary but a "socially acquired inheritance" that develops as "social as well as physical," but that the "social needs and aims have been the most potent in shaping it."[35] For Dewey—and William James before him—the mind is "essentially a process," one in which "there is a process of growth, not a fixed thing."[36]

The Dewey metaphor that best describes his philosophy of education with its boundless optimism and its lack of a dark side is as follows:

"The school building . . . ought to be in a garden, and the children from the garden would be led on to surrounding fields, and then into the wider country, with all its facts and forces."[37] This bucolic scenario is free from poverty and its correlates—crime, drugs, joblessness, cramped living conditions, and hunger. This short passage reveals both the beauty and limitation of Dewey's vision. Where *The School and Society* falters is in the vagueness of Dewey's social aims. Dewey's liberal democratic socialist impulses became well known in time, but he failed to give a specific recipe for how to go about reconstructing society through schooling. Dewey was clear in how to reorganize the school experience, but he was less clear bout its relationship to restructuring society.

Others concur. Richard Pratte criticized Dewey for not "possessing a grand strategy for transforming American schools into institutions working on behalf of radical change."[38] For Pratte, the bottom line was political and social change. He found Dewey's vague references to a social impulse lacking in both programmatic ideas and organized efforts. He reached this conclusion despite Dewey's lifelong espousal of liberal causes. He charged that "Dewey was no Martin Luther King, Jr. Dr. King, unlike Dewey, took to the streets with both a vision and a strategy. . . . After having identified and described white privilege, he outlined and followed a strategy to end it."[39]

The fault was that Dewey had no concrete ideas about how to go about transforming American corporate capitalism. Pratte summed up:

despite his eloquent plea for democratic socialism (a grand vision), Dewey's thinking remained bereft of a grand *program of action*. . . . Although he wanted to tear down corporate capitalism and substitute democratic socialism, he was not at all clear about what was to be done as the first step toward democratic control of the economy [emphasis added].[40]

In Dewey's defense, he was primarily a philosopher with an educational bent, rather than a political strategist. He had a deep faith in democracy and education and felt that each could aid the other. In short, Dewey's political tool for transforming society was the schools. The schools would be the change agents. By the 1970s, some social critics of the left and right perceived the schools to be, in Christopher Jencks description, "marginal institutions" that merely replicated the social order rather than provide social mobility. Jencks admonished egalitarians to "establish political control over the economic institutions that shape our society."[41] In short, when the schools fell out of favor as change agents, Dewey's call for the transformation of society through the schools also appeared outdated.

In *Schools of To-Morrow*, co-written with his daughter, Evelyn, Dewey presented an example of his progressive ideas at work. This account of his laboratory school at the University of Chicago continued his generous optimism on learning through experience. First, Dewey insisted that "children should enjoy school."[42] Moreover, school must be a place "where children work together" since "the child must learn to work with others."[43] Dewey elaborated: "The more closely and more directly the child learns by entering into social situations the more genuine and effective the knowledge he gains."[44]

The progressive school of tomorrow, then, offered freedom, individuality, and play in the curriculum. Again it is the vagueness of Dewey's strictures on social relations that gave rise to misunderstanding by his followers and criticism by postmodern educators. Consider this passage from *The School and Society*: "the primary business of school is to train children to co-operation and mutually helpful living; to foster in them the consciousness of mutual independence; and to help them practically in making the *adjustment* that will carry this spirit into overt deeds" (emphasis added).[45] It is understandable, therefore, that a sympathetic critic such as Lawrence Cremin would perceive in Dewey's thought the seeds of an educational program that mainly stressed adjusting to society. Cremin concluded that: "however tortuous the intellectual line from democracy and education to the pronouncements of the Commission on Life Adjustment Education, that line can be drawn."[46]

Other scholars have distanced Dewey from the excesses of the progressive education movement. Phillip S. Riner argued that although Dewey "did influence the progressive school movement . . . the movement was always beyond his control."[47] For Riner, the progressive education movement absorbed Dewey's ideas, then proceeded on its own path. He concluded that: "Dewey had great difficulty embodying his ideas into educational practice, particularly in directing the reformist movement toward a scientific experimentalist posture. The progressive movement was never an embodiment of Dewey's ideal or the source of his legacy. . . . Each chose to interpret Dewey's teachings in his or her own way."[48]

British scholar R. S. Peters added that Dewey "was not a wholehearted supporter of the progressive movement in America."[49] There is some evidence for this view. Dewey criticized "the negative aspect of progressive education" as early as 1930—ten years after the formation of the Progressive Education Association.[50] Dewey was uncomfortable with the "unrestrained freedom of action and speech" he found in some progressive schools that approached "the point of anarchy."[51] For Dewey, "a truly progressive school should maintain genuine control of experiences that are intrinsically worthwhile by objective subject matter . . . [so that] excessive liberty of outward action will also be registered."[52]

Even Revisionist historian Joel Spring considered Dewey apart from other progressive educators. In *Education and the Rise of the Corporate State*,

Spring argued that Dewey was grossly misinterpreted so that his emphasis on society to develop a sense of community was translated into simple life adjustment.

DEWEY'S CRITICS

The criticism against Dewey reached the highest levels of U.S. society. While president and after Sputnik, Dwight D. Eisenhower blamed America's allegedly inferior educational system squarely on John Dewey. In a letter written five months after the Soviet Union launched the first spaceship, Eisenhower denounced Dewey's influence:

educators, parents and students alike must be continuously stirred up by the defects in our educational system. They must be induced to abandon the educational path that, rather blindly, they have been following as a result of John Dewey's teachings . . . .[W]hen he [or his followers] went freewheeling into the realm of basic education they, in my opinion, did a great disservice to the American public.[53]

Eisenhower's letter was published a year later, in 1959, in the pages of *Life* magazine, the most popular magazine of its day for the general public. An ironic note was that, immediately prior to the presidency, Eisenhower was president of Columbia University, the university long associated with Dewey.

The Sputnik crisis produced n the United States a wave of hysteria during the height of the Cold War. The Soviet Union's lead in space panicked America into seeking educational reform to shore up its scientific brainpower. The emphasis was on basics. Progressive education— and its chief protagonist John Dewey—was the culprit held responsible for the supposed educational decline. U.S. senators would accuse progressive educators for "stunting the growth of young Americans."[54] A consistent critic was Admiral Hyman Rickover, known for his role in the development of the first atomic submarine. Rickover would scorn progressive education for not being "nearly as difficult as teaching algebra, French, or physics."[55] Eisenhower would echo the call to a "return to fundamentals," which would "stress English, history, mathematics, the simply rudiments of one or more of the sciences, and at least one language."[56] Indeed, Eisenhower's sympathetic biographer, Stephen E. Ambrose, felt that Eisenhower had "a great opportunity wasted" that he "could have used . . . to vastly strengthen the educational system in the United States."[57]

The Sputnik crisis signaled the beginning of the end for the influence of progressive education. But Dewey and his colleagues, in truth, were under fire from traditionalists from the start. The attacks intensified from religious conservatives in the 1930s, from conservative educators in the 1940s and 1950s, and, ironically, from leftist critics in the 1960s and 1970s.

Dewey's severest critics were religious. Roman Catholic Jesuit scholar Neil G. McCluskey would score Dewey's educational philosophy for the lack of a moral perspective in his 1958 book, *Public Schools and Moral Education.* According to McCluskey, Dewey "made a religion out of education."[58] And education for Dewey, McCluskey maintained, was to reconstruct society. In that regard, McCluskey chided Dewey for merely urging churches to "stimulate action for a divine kingdom."[59] Dewey's acknowledgement of "intellectual sustenance" in addressing social problems was held against him.[60]

Consequently, McCluskey perceived that Dewey's influence, in effect, shortchanged American public schools. "For millions of American families," McCluskey concluded, "the public school system as presently constructed is simply incapable of caring for the moral side of education."[61] One can perceive in this argument a brief for parochial schools. Moreover, McCluskey confused moral with religious—two not necessarily equivalent concepts. Surely Dewey's emphasis on the social, on human compassion, is of a high moral nature; it is admittedly not necessarily religious.

Other religious attacks on Dewey were not as genteel. Dewey was not only derided for his atheism; his patriotism and love of democracy were also questioned. He was accused of being "un-American," promoting "totalitarianism in the clothing of democracy."[62] Again the attacks were from Roman Catholic conservatives and came as early as 1939. At the National Catholic Alumni Federation conference in that year, Father Geoffrey O'Connell accused Dewey of destroying "Christian aims and ideals in American education"[63]—the reason: Dewey's atheism. According to O'Connell, Dewey "ignores God, the supernatural, religion, the Ten Commandments, the eternal moral law, the soul, immortality, everything, in fact, which is above and beyond the purely imperial realm of existence."[64]

Another speaker at the conference, an associate editor of *The Wall Street Journal,* charged Dewey with eliminating from the public school curriculum "the one thing upon which our whole theory of government and elemental liberties depend, namely religion."[65]

These attacks regularly appeared in *The Tablet,* an ultraconservative Catholic diocesan paper published in Brooklyn, New York. A Catholic physician accused Dewey of "poisoning the minds of our youth."[66] A Catholic judge saw Dewey's "dominant philosophy of secular education" as a "menace to American youth." He declared "Why do we need to look farther for the causes of the alarming prevalence and steady increase of crime and juvenile delinquency . . . [than the] pagan philosophy of [John Dewey].[67]

For the most part, such religious attacks on Dewey were buried with him. In some cases, there has been a lingering uneasiness. One Catholic, a former New York school superintendent, who received his doctorate at Teachers College and devoted his life to public schools, still felt in 1992 "prejudiced against Dewey's thinking because he was an atheist."[68] And the failed attempts at passing a constitutional amendment for school prayer by presidents Reagan and Bush reflected this antipathy toward public schools.

From the left, Dewey was accused of an educational philosophy that was the basis of inequality. These revisionists believed that progressivism in education mainly reinforced America's stratified capitalist system. They concluded that Dewey's inattention to the unique problems of educating the poor revealed the limitations of his progressive vision. Still others perceived a direct line from Dewey to the revisionist critics. They would argue that "the generation of young Americans of the 1960s" who took up "the work of educational and social change" were "the philosophical descendants of John Dewey."[69]

DEWEY'S INFLUENCE

John Dewey not only gave American education its essential character, but he influenced educational systems abroad. Internationally, Dewey's ideas were incorporated in some unlikely places. His lectures in the early part of the twentieth century in Japan and China proclaimed the progressive gospel. As a result, according to his biographer, "Dewey's philosophy of education was the dominant one in China" until the 1949 Communist revolution.[70] Understandably, Dewey "became the main target" of the Communists. He was denounced by a Communist functionary for that "poisonous Pragmatic philosophy spread over China . . . primarily through his lectures in China . . . and through that center of Dewey's reactionary thinking, namely, Columbia University, from which thousands of Chinese students . . . have brought back all the reactionary . . . Pragmatic educational ideas of Dewey."[71]

In Japan, ironically, some of Dewey's ideas are still felt. One American educator commented that "if I had $1000 for every time a Japanese teacher has described her practices to me and mentions John Dewey, I'd be a wealthy person."[72]

As for the United States, scholarly opinion is divided on Dewey's influence. Some believe his ideas are still evident in American classrooms. Others conclude that no American public school follows his ideas on curriculum. Still others find Dewey's philosophy more prevalent in private schools. And, finally, there are those who believe that the "time . . . [is] right for another Dewey revival."[73]

What is incontrovertible is the interest in John Dewey's work. Dewey's major books on education—including *Democracy and Education, The School and Society,* and *The Child and the Curriculum*—are still in print. These books have been translated into thirty-five languages. The scholarly journal *Critical Thinking* embodies Dewey's major concept. Educational journals have averaged seven articles yearly on Dewey in the decade 1982 to 1992, many of which have been in the philosophical journal *Educational Theory.*

Most important, Dewey has been consulted on current educational disputes. Like the great books throughout history—the Bible, the Koran, the works of Marx and Freud—Dewey is constantly being reinterpreted to fix the educational controversies of the day. Never mind that these questions—much less answers—were not part of Dewey's era. Dewey's educational philosophy has been mined to shed light on such disparate topics as feminism and education, the revision of the literary canon in the universities, and his thought on Jewish education. As one scholar expressed it: "I do not think a discussion of American education should be conducted without taking seriously what John Dewey said about it. His is the most sustained and deepest thinking any American has ever done about education."[74]

Let us consider the issue of Dewey and feminism. In recent years, a number of feminist scholars have sought support in Dewey's work. One such scholar considered Dewey's work to be comprised of "a sophisticated theoretical feminism."[75] Another claimed that Dewey's private letters indicated leanings toward feminist causes. Others, however, argued that Dewey "never publicly claimed feminism."[76] Yet they believed that if Dewey were alive, he would rally to feminist banners.

Another controversy is that of the "canon," multiculturalism, and the revision of literary works. The "canon" is the idea that there are texts of outstanding literary merit that are essential readings for the educated person. The idea of a canon originated with the southern literary New Critics of the 1940s such as Allen Tate. The canon has come under severe scrutiny in the last decade by revisionists who argue that these literary works only include white, male, and European-American authors. These revisionist scholars argue for a more inclusive group to writers who represent minority, female, and non-European or non-American writers. They base their revised canon both on literary merit and sociological interest.

Professor William Shea consulted Dewey's writings on the idea of a canon and concluded that "Dewey *seemed opposed* to lists of required classics and perhaps to the very notion of a classic" (emphasis added).[77] Shea based his argument on Dewey's opposition to Robert Maynard Hutchins's Great Books concept. Hutchins was the youngest president of the University of Chicago and a staunch defender of classical education. Hutchins proposed that college courses should encompass the great books of civilization. In his words, Hutchins advocated a "general education course of study consisting of the great books of the western world."[78] Dewey was uneasy with this concept. In reviewing one of Hutchins's books he disliked the idea because it seemed a "distrust of freedom."[79] For Dewey, the essential problem was "who is to determine the definite truths that constitute the hierarchy" of great books.[80] Writing in 1937, with fascism on the rise, Dewey went so far as to imply that Hutchins's great books idea was totalitarian. "Dewey has stated my position in such a way as to lead me to think that I cannot write," Hutchins replied, "and has stated his own in such a way as to make me suspect that I cannot read."[81]

The episode convinced Shea that if Dewey were alive he would say that "with a canon . . . democracy is finished."[82] Surely Dewey, ever the relativist, was suspicious of anything presented as immutable. On the other hand, speculation on how Dewey would react in a postmodern multicultural society may prove to be a futile enterprise. But it is a tribute to Dewey's staying power that today's scholars feel the need to consult him.

CONCLUSION

What do we conclude about John Dewey? First, he was the first major American philosopher who gave education in the United States its distinctive character. His key ideas of developing critical thinking, whole child development, and relating knowledge to experience formed an educational infrastructure that is uniquely American. Indeed, Dewey casts such a large shadow that few philosophers have followed in his footsteps. One British scholar related the story of how he attempted to interest "an eminent American philosopher" to pursue "the philosophy of education." That gray eminence replied that Dewey had "killed the subject stone dead."[83]

But Dewey was a child of his age. Lawrence Cremin summed up Dewey's contribution as great but saddled "with the problem of anachronism."[84] For Cremin, Dewey's writings were "steeped in the thought of early twentieth century urban progressivism."[85] Cremin concluded that Dewey "must be seen as of a genre with . . . Thorsten Veblen, Jane Addams and Jacob Riis."[86] What is needed at the moment is another John Dewey to add to the infrastructure of American educational thought.

NOTES

1. George Dykhuizen, *The Life and Mind of John Dewey* (Carbondale: Southern Illinois University Press, 1973), p. xiv.
2. *Ibid.*, p. 12.

3. *Ibid.*, p. 21.

4. *Ibid.*, p. 249.

5. *Ibid.*, p. 97.

6. *Ibid.*

7. Richard Pratt, "Reconsiderations," *Educational Studies*, Summer 1992, p. 139.

8. Dykhuizen, *John Dewey*, p. 88.

9. John Dewey, "Professional Organization of Teachers," *American Teacher*, September 1916, p. 99.

10. *Ibid.*, p. 101.

11. Dykhuizen, *John Dewey*, p. xxii.

12. Pratte, "Reconsiderations," p. 139.

13. David A. Shannon, *The Socialist Party of America* (Chicago: Quadrangle Books, 1955), p. 5.

14. Dykhuizen, *John Dewey*, p. 118.

15. Interview with Bob Nelson, Public Information Officer, Columbia University, New York City, December 16, 1993 (telephone).

16. John Dewey, *Democracy and Education* (New York: The Macmillan Co., 1931), p. v.

17. *Ibid.*, p. 98.

18. *Ibid.*, p. 101.

19. *Ibid.*

20. *Ibid.*, p. 31.

21. *Ibid.*, p. 14.

22. *Ibid.*, p. 188.

23. *Ibid.*, p. 222.

24. *Ibid.*, p. 188.

25. *Ibid.*

26. *Ibid.*, p. 246.

27. *Ibid.*, p. 261.

28. *Ibid.*, p. 402.

29. *Ibid.*

30. *Ibid.*, p. 411.

31. John Dewey, *The School and Society* (Chicago: University of Chicago Press, 1900), p. 4.

32. *Ibid.*

33. *Ibid.*, p. 9.

34. *Ibid.*

35. *Ibid.*, p. 91.

36. *Ibid.*, p. 94.

37. *Ibid.*, p. 67.

38. Pratte, "Reconsiderations," p. 141.

39. *Ibid.*, pp. 148–149.

40. *Ibid.*, p. 147.

41. Christopher Jencks et al., *Inequality* (New York: Basic Books, 1973), p. 265.

42. John Dewey and Evelyn Dewey, *Schools of To-Morrow* (New York: E. P. Dutton, 1915), p. 41.

43. *Ibid.*, p. 20.

44. *Ibid.*, p. 63.
45. Dewey, *The School and Society*, pp. 111–112.
46. Lawrence Cremin, *The Transformation of the School: Progressivism in American Education 1876–1957* (New York: Vintage, 1961), p. 239.
47. Phillip S. Riner, "Dewey's Legacy to Education," *The Educational Forum*, Winter 1989, p. 186.
48. *Ibid.*, pp. 186–187.
49. R. S. Peters, "John Dewey's Philosophy of Education," in *John Dewey Reconsidered*, edited by R. S. Peters (London: Routledge and Kegan Paul, 1977), p. 103.
50. John Dewey, "How Much Freedom in New Schools?" *The New Republic*, July 9, 1930, p. 204.
51. *Ibid.*, p. 205.
52. *Ibid.*
53. Dwight D. Eisenhower, "The Private Letters of the President," *Life*, March 16, 1959, p. 114.
54. *New York Times*, November 14, 1957, p. 20.
55. Hyman G. Rickover, *Education and Freedom* (New York: E. P. Dutton, 1959), p. 136.
56. Eisenhower, "Private Letters," p. 114.
57. Stephen E. Ambrose, *Eisenhower: The President*, vol. 2 (New York: Simon and Schuster, 1983), p. 460.
58. Neil G. McCluskey, *Public Schools and Moral Education* (New York: Columbia University Press, 1958), p. 253.
59. *Ibid.*, p. 229.
60. *Ibid.*, p. 184.
61. *Ibid.*, p. 271.
62. *New York Times*, October 27, 1939, p. 14.
63. *Ibid.*
64. *Ibid.*
65. *Ibid.*
66. *The Tablet*, December 16, 1939, p. 14.
67. *The Tablet*, December 2, 1939, p. 15.
68. Interview with Joseph P. Mooney, former Superintendent of Schools, Uniondale, Long Island, Virginia Beach, Va., June 9, 1992.
69. Harold Taylor, "Introduction," in Dykhuizen, *John Dewey*, p. xxiv.
70. Dykhuizen, *John Dewey*, p. 204.
71. *Ibid.*
72. *New York Times*, April 26, 1992, p. E5.
73. Emily Robertson, "Is Dewey's Educational Vision Still Viable?" in *Review of Research in Education 18*, edited by Gerald D. Grant (Washington, D.C.: American Educational Research Association, 1992), p. 337.
74. William M. Shea, "John Dewey and the Crisis of the Canon," *American Journal of Education*, May 1989, p. 293.
75. Susan Laird, "Women and Gender in John Dewey's Philosophy of Education," *Educational Theory*, Winter 1988, p. 112.
76. *Ibid.*
77. William M. Shea, "John Dewey," p. 289.

78. *Ibid.*, p. 219.
79. *Ibid.*
80. *Ibid.*
81. *Ibid.*
82. *Ibid.*, p. 294.
83. Riner, "Dewey's Legacy," p. 112.
84. Cremin, *The Transformation*, p. 238.
85. *Ibid.*, p. 239.
86. *Ibid.*

CHAPTER FOUR

THE CIVIL RIGHTS MOVEMENT AND EQUITY REFORM

In her history of American education after World War II, *The Troubled Crusade,* historian Diane Ravitch characterized the educational reform movement that took place in the 1960s as a "new progressivism." This "new progressivism," Ravitch wrote, "grew out of a bitter reaction against the inadequacies of the American public schools in educating minority children."[1] The decade of the 1960s was to witness the second major educational reform movement in American history—one which I dub the equity reform movement—and it was shaped by the Civil Rights Movement.

The emergence of a massive Civil Rights Movement between 1954 and 1968 was the major domestic event in American politics. And it had indelible influence in determining a national educational agenda for nearly a generation. Meyer Weinberg, a historian of school desegregation, argued that the Civil Rights Movement was "the principal engine for educational change in this country."[2] U.S. Commission of Education in the Johnson administration, Francis Keppel, in addressing the American Association of School Administrators in 1964 linked the pressure of the Civil Rights Movement for educational change with an emergent equity educational reform movement:

The spirit of our times convinces me that we are now given a chance which does not come often to the educational community . . . that we can truly bring equal opportunity to the schools of poverty. . . .

Of all the pressures we now feel which tend to evoke our defenses . . . the most acute is the civil rights movement. . . . I say: Thank God for the civil rights movement. It provides the very opportunity we have been looking for.[3]

Civil rights leaders understood the value of education for African Americans in order to succeed in American life. Education became a major issue for the Civil Rights Movement. Moreover, civil rights leaders perceived the U.S. public school system as one that could more easily be influenced by legislation, court decisions, or street protests. Community control theorist/activist Preston R. Wilcox declared that "a confrontation has occurred between the Black and/or poor and the school system," and that resulted in "a revolutionary view of the role of the school in the community."[4]

The success of the civil rights leaders in securing change in education varied. They emphasized three broad avenues: desegregation of public schools, community control of schools and the installation of Afrocentric curriculums, and affirmative action policies that provided educational access to blacks and other minorities. (We shall examine the community control movement, of which I was a part, in the next chapter). This agenda energized an educational reform movement that was codified in national policies by the Kennedy and Johnson administrations. We shall examine the influence of the Civil Rights Movement, and we will consult the educational ideas and emphasis on education of three major African-American civil rights leaders: W.E.B. DuBois, Rev. Martin Luther King, Jr., and Malcolm X.

BLACK LEADERS ON EDUCATION

African-American leaders from Booker T. Washington to Jesse Jackson have stressed the importance of education. Although they have reached consensus on the need for educational opportunities for black students, they have often diverged on specific strategies to achieve these goals. Of the three civil rights leaders' views on education to be discussed, W.E.B. DuBois predated the rise of the modern Civil Rights Movement but set the stage for what was to follow; Rev. Martin Luther King, Jr., projected an educational strategy that was more conventional, whereas his contemporary Malcolm X stressed ideas such as an Afrocentric curriculum that have import a generation after his death. Both DuBois and King, whose formal education was superior to that of Malcolm X, revealed a debt to progressive thinkers.

W.E.B. DuBois and Integration

Of the three, W.E.B. DuBois was a genuine scholar, the author of innumerable books and articles on race in America. Born in 1868 in Massachusetts, of Haitian extraction, DuBois lived nearly 100 years. Raised primarily by his grandfather, a middle-class grocery store owner and occasional poet, DuBois always believed that he would attend college.

"In my mind," he wrote in his autobiography, "there was no doubt I was going to college."[5] He had set his sights on Harvard. However, his high school's academic reputation was deemed insufficient for him to enter Harvard. With extra financial help from three white community leaders (two high school principals and a congregational pastor) he attended Fisk University in Atlanta, Georgia. Graduating from Fisk, he applied to Harvard. Harvard, however, did not recognize a Fisk degree, and he had to start over as an undergraduate. The pattern was repeated when he attended the University of Berlin, which, in turn, regarded Harvard as part of an educational and cultural American wasteland.

At Harvard, he came under the influence of William James who "guided [him] . . . to realist pragmatism."[6] DuBois was to become "repeatedly a guest in the house of William James; he was my friend and guide to clear thinking."[7] At Harvard and the University of Berlin he was, as a black man, odd man out. At Fisk, an all-black college, he perceived the strength of black schools for blacks, and he preached the virtues of black colleges.

DuBois became an academic, teaching at various colleges such as Wilberforce, the University of Pennsylvania, and Atlanta University. He left academic life to pursue a career as an activist/scholar. DuBois's first foray into social activism was as founder of the Niagara movement. The Niagara movement was a forming of a small, select group of blacks who declared their commitment to an "organized determination and aggressive action on the part of men who believe in Negro freedom and growth."[8] A few years later, he would join the staff of the fledgling National Association for the Advancement of Colored People (NAACP), then a biracial group, determined to fight racism mainly through legal channels. DuBois was the NAACP director of publications and research from 1910 to 1934, founding the journal *Crisis*. He would return to the NAACP for a four-year period between 1944 and 1948. DuBois joined the Communist Party and lived out his last years in Africa.

DuBois's key educational and social philosophy was to develop an elite of African Americans, a "Talented Tenth who through their knowledge of modern culture could guide the American Negro into higher education."[9] His importance in this study was his emphasis on the value of black schooling given the racist context in the United States. DuBois was not optimistic about prospects for school integration, either its eventuality or, in the case of it becoming fact, its benefits for blacks in a society deeply ingrained with racism. Consequently, his arguments for the preservation of black schools and colleges with their attendant black teachers raised the question of what would best serve African Americans in the long run.

DuBois presented his ideas in a famed 1935 article, "Does the Negro Need Separate Schools?" First, he doubted whether school integration would be beneficial given deep-seated racism. "Race prejudice in the United States today," he charged, "is such that most Negroes cannot receive proper education in white institutions."[10] Indeed, he argued, blacks in public schools "are not educated; they are crucified."[11]

Second, DuBois feared the dissipation of black culture in white institutions. "Negroes must know the history of the Negro race in America," he pleaded, "and this they will seldom get in white institutions."[12] He chided African Americans for a lack of belief in their own capabilities:

at the bottom [is] an utter lack of faith on the part of Negroes that their race can do anything really well. If Negroes could conceive that Negroes could establish schools quite as good as or even superior to white schools . . . then separation would be a passing incident and not a permanent evil; but as long as American Negroes believe that their race is constitutionally and permanently inferior to white people, they necessarily disbelieve in every possible Negro institution.[13]

DuBois anticipated the Black Power movement of the 1960s with its emphasis on black pride. Moreover, he hinted at the community control movement, an offshoot of Black Power, that sought control of ghetto schooling by black parents. "It is for this reason that when our schools are separated the control of the teaching force, the expenditure of money, the choice of textbooks, the discipline and other administrative matters of this sort ought, also, to come into our hands, and be incessantly demanded and guarded."[14]

With the *Brown v. Topeka Board of Education* ruling of the U.S. Supreme Court outlawing segregated schools in 1954, DuBois modified his views. He argued that blacks must "accept equality or die" since "by the law of the land today" schools must be desegregated.[15] However, he warned of a possible negative fallout from desegregation. "If and when [blacks] are admitted" to integrated schools, he feared that "Negro teachers will become rarer and in many cases will disappear . . . .Theoretically Negro universities will disappear . . . [and] Negro history will be taught less or not at all."[16]

For DuBois desegregation was a two-edged sword. On the one hand, he hoped for "the utter disapperance of color discrimination in American life."[17] On the other hand, he was steadfast in mainstreaming "the preservation of African history and culture."[18]

DuBois's fears of a black brain drain of students and teachers to white institutions were far from unfounded. By the 1990s, many African-American educators bemoaned the drift of black students away from teaching to more lucrative occupations and of black students to white colleges and universities. However, an emphasis within public and private schools and colleges on African-American culture did not disappear. Black history month has become an annual event in February in schools and colleges. Textbooks have been revised to include the black experience in America. Black studies programs and departments have been created at many universities, cresting by the mid-1970s. DuBois was correct, however, in understanding that integration posed a dilemma to African Americans.

Rev. Martin Luther King, Jr., and Desegregation

Rev. Martin Luther King, Jr., overcame mostly segregated public schooling to eventually excel in higher education. The son of a college-educated minister comfortably established as the pastor of a large Atlanta church, Ebenezzer Baptist, King skipped the ninth and twelfth grades at segregated Booker T. Washington High School. However, his public school education did not fully prepare him for Morehouse College, a black institution that was his father's alma mater. At Morehouse, King averaged a mediocre C, and the college president regarded him one of the "good minds" but not one of "the brilliant students."[19] Still, he saw potential in the young King and noted that King had "come to realize the value of scholarship late in his career."[20]

At Crozer Theological Seminary, King came into full academic bloom. His major professor considered King as someone with "exceptional intellectual ability."[21] It was at Crozer that King first encountered the writings of the Social Gospel advocate Walter Rauschenbusch. Enthused by Rauschenbusch's social vision, King proceeded to study the works of the theologian Reinhold Niebur, the economic historian R. H. Tawney, and the pacifist social activists A. J. Muste and Mahatma Ghandi. King went on to Boston University for a doctorate in theology after graduating from Crozer.

King's educational message was threefold. First, he perceived education as an essential part of his vision of social reconstruction. Second, he believed in integrated education. And third, he advocated educational remedies that were, for the most part, traditional. King's program for social change, with education as a key ingredient, was grounded in the thinking of the progressives.

King understood the connection between education and social mobility for African Americans. Although he failed to mention education in his most famous utterance—the "I Have a Dream" speech of the 1963 March on Washington—his writings stressed education. In the March on Washington speech, King emphasized desegregation, poverty, and voting rights.

In his books and articles, such as his last book, *Where Do We Go From Here?* education was prominent. "The schools have been the historic routes of social mobility," he wrote, "but when Negroes and others of the underclass now ask that the schools lay the same function for them, many . . . answer that the schools cannot do the job."²² For those who argued that a child's family background was the primary determinant of educational success, King had a ready answer. "The job of the school," King maintained, "is to teach so well that family background is no longer an issue."²³ Citing the U.S. Office of Education 1966 study of education, commonly called the Coleman Report, King wrote that "while integrated education *does not* retard white students," there was no doubt in his mind that the evidence showed that school integration "does improve the performance of the Negro."²⁴

King's program for school improvement, in addition to school desegregation, contained few new ideas or, for that matter, ideas specifically concerned with the education of African Americans. He called for "more money" for schools and to help "teachers to teach more effectively" and to develop a "new and creative link between parents and schools."²⁵ But King nibbled at the educational ideas of Black Power advocates such as Malcolm X. Although denouncing Black Power as a "nihilistic philosophy born out of the conviction that the Negro can't win," King acknowledged "the right of all parents . . . to have a significant role in educational decisions affecting their children"—a key demand of the community control Black Power advocates.²⁶ Moreover, King criticized textbooks that "ignore the Negro's contribution to American life" since his children and all black children . . . have been denied a knowledge of their heritage."²⁷ But King would not go so far as DuBois or Malcolm X in endorsing an Afrocentric curriculum. The key to King's vision of social reconstruction was not education but economic equality. From that concept, he believed the other "piecemeal" reforms would benefit. For King, "the simplest approach" to equality for blacks was full employment and a guaranteed income.²⁸

There was much in King's thoughts that echoed the progressives. Joseph Carpenter demonstrated in his study of King's philosophy similarities between King and such progressive education reformers as George S. Counts. For Carpenter, King's proposition that "the school take the lead in changing the social order" resembled Counts's challenge in his book *Dare the School Build a New Social Order?*²⁹ King's debunking of several "educational myths" in an article on integration was very similar to "ten basic fallacies" concerning education discussed by Counts in his book.³⁰ Moreover, Carpenter argued further that King's educational philosophy was identical to that of Dewey, Counts, and others on the purpose of schooling: that, as King wrote, "intelligence is not enough" and the "goal of education" is "intelligence plus character."³¹

Malcolm X and Black Culture

Another African-American leader to emphasize education was Malcolm X. Son of a minister killed by the Klu Klux Klan, Malcolm drifted into foster homes, a life of crime and prison, and eventual survival through the nation of Islam religion. A precocious youngster, Malcolm's academic potential was recognized by some white teachers who offered him "advice about how to become something in life."[32] In the seventh grade, his marks "were the highest in school."[33] In the nearly all-white school, Malcolm was elected class president, perhaps because as the sole black he was "unique in my class, like a pink poodle."[34]

As he evolved into a brilliant orator against racism, Malcolm wished he had the opportunity for college. He informed his biographer Alex Haley that "My greatest lack has been, I believe, that I don't have the kind of academic education I wish I had been able to get....I would not be one bit ashamed to go back into any New York City public school and start where I left off at the ninth grade, and go on through a degree. Because I don't begin to be academically equipped for so many of the interests that I have."[35]

His ambition was "to have been a lawyer" because he always "loved verbal battle."[36] It is with some irony that this charismatic speaker, second only to Barry Goldwater in being invited for college speaking engagements, would address Harvard Law School and look through the lecture hall window "in the direction of the apartment house that was my old burglary gang's hideout."[37]

Malcolm was self-taught. During his seven-year prison term, he began his studies. First, he read the dictionary from A to Z so that he could learn the words. Soon he was in the "new world" of books and "in every free moment" he was either "reading in the library ... [or] reading in my bunk."[38] His "alma mater was books," and he familiarized himself with an eclectic group of authors ranging from Schopenhauer to Shakespeare.[39]

Consequently, Malcolm X was a friend to education. At the heart of racism he charged was "inferior housing, inferior employment, inferior education."[40] Racism meant that blacks were given "a segregated school system which gives inferior education."[41] Racial oppression meant that whites

very skillfully [do this] to keep us trapped. They know that as long as they keep us undereducated, or with an inferior education, it's impossible for us to compete with them for job openings. And as long as we can't compete with them and get a decent job, we're trapped. We are low-wage earners. We have to live in a run down neighborhood, which means our children go to inferior schools. They get inferior education.... And when they grow up, they fall right into the same cycle again.[42]

Malcolm's solution was an earlier version of community control where blacks determine school policy including curriculum. In the platform of the Organization for Afro-American Unity that he formed after leaving the Nation of Islam, Malcolm outlined his educational program. The "basic unity program" called for African Americans to "completely control our own education institutions."[43] In addition, the accent would be on an Afrocentric curriculum so that blacks could "influence the choice of textbooks and equipment used by our children in public schools" and to encourage "qualified Afro-Americans to write and publish the textbooks to liberate our minds."[44]

THE STRUGGLE FOR DESEGREGATED SCHOOLS

The first major effort toward securing educational opportunity for African Americans was to desegregate the public schools. Culminating in the historic *Brown* decision, efforts at desegregation, led by the NAACP, underlined the importance of education for American blacks. The deplorable conditions of segregated public schools was a moral, political, and educational issue. Morally, school integration was a basic human right: to have the same access to schooling not denied because of color. Politically, school integration tested the fabric of a democratic society. Educationally, school integration held the promise of benefitting African-American students in terms of academic achievement.

Whether school integration has educationally aided blacks has been debated. Supporters argue that school integration has provided better education for black students. Reviewing a generation of school desegregation studies, African-American scholar Charles V. Willie declared that "school desegregation has contributed to the enhancement of education in this nation more than any other experience in recent years."[45] Another supporter Robert A. Dentler contended that school desegregation has the "potential, simply, to improve a youth's chances, to enable him or her to move more confidently and with self-esteem through the occupational and political realms that whites dominate."[46] Critics of school integration, such as David Armor, have argued that school integration has not increased the academic performance of black students.[47] The results of various studies, thus, have been mixed. However, a review of a great number of such studies indicates that school integration has been on balance beneficial to black students in terms of school performance.

World War II proved to be a watershed for civil rights leaders concerning the education of blacks. Forty percent of the nation's pupils were in segregated schools at that time.[48] More important, resources available to black schools suffered by comparison with those given to white schools. In the South, more than twice the amount of money spent on the education of black children was spent on the schooling of whites. White teachers were paid 30 percent more money than black teachers at these schools.[49]

With the passage of the G.I. Bill of Rights in 1944 and the return of African-American war veterans, the pressure to open white colleges and universities to blacks increased. Few black institutions offered graduate or professional degrees. Only two black universities had medical schools, and none had doctoral programs.[50] An overflow of black applicants to graduate schools convinced leaders of the NAACP to attempt to gain access to these schools.

The NAACP's Legal and Education Defense Fund succeeded in a number of court cases in obtaining admissions to a number of these graduate schools through legal challenges. These successes emboldened NAACP leaders to attack the problem of school integration wholesale. The constitutional problem was to mount a campaign to reverse the 1896 U.S. Supreme Court decision in *Plessy vs. Ferguson* that legitimized separate but equal schooling. The chief attorney for the Legal and Education Defense Fund was Thurgood Marshall. Convinced that by the early 1950s the NAACP had reached a crossroads in pursuing racial equality, Marshall argued that the time was opportune to challenge the constitutional basis of segregation. He called a policy conference with leading civil rights lawyers and constitutional law professors on the topic "to end segregation once and for all."[51] That conference was followed with another comprised of forty-three lawyers and fourteen regional NAACP presidents in June 1950. Marshall allayed the fears of some that efforts to dismantle public school desegregation would aid and set back civil rights efforts. The group followed Marshall's lead and declared NAACP policy that in the future all education cases would "be aimed at obtaining education on a non-segregated basis and that no relief other than that will be acceptable. . . . Further, that all lawyers operating under such rule will urge their client[s] and the branches of the Association on this final relief."[52] It was a bold and decisive move that would eventually change segregation and America.

The U.S. Supreme Court decision to outlaw school segregation marked the beginning of the major phase of the modern Civil Rights Movement. Beyond its legal ramifications, the decision energized African-American leaders to supplement the legal tactics of the NAACP with direct mass protest in the streets. The culmination of this two-pronged effort was the civil rights and the voting rights acts in the 1960s.

But the decision had legal implications. For the first time, a major constitutional case, the *Brown* decision, was determined on the basis of sociological and psychological evidence rather than merely legal precedent. This new emphasis prompted a counteroffensive by conservatives who argue to this day for judicial restraint—that is, to mainly adhere to legal precedent. Marshall and the NAACP legal staff decided to base their case mostly on psychological research with black school children, termed the "doll study." The doll study was conducted by African-

American psychologists Kenneth and Mamie Clark. They had first published their results in 1940 in the *Journal of Experimental Education* and recycled their evidence for a monograph at the 1950 White House Conference on Children and Youth. It was the latter that caught the attention of Marshall.

The design of the doll study was simple. The study was conducted in Boston and Worcester, Massachusetts; Philadelphia; and several cities in Arkansas. Preschool black children ranging in age from 3 to 7 were presented with four identical-looking dolls, two brown and two white. They were asked which they preferred playing with, which they found to be the "nice" doll, and which they considered to have a "nice" color. A majority of the black children preferred the white doll. The Clarks concluded that there was "an unmistakable preference for the white doll and a rejection of the brown doll," and they interpreted segregation as a "factor in the racial identification of Negro pre-school children" that resulted in lower self-esteem and lower academic performance.[53]

Criticism of the doll study has continued to the present day despite a successful replication in the mid-1980s by two different scholars. Conservative legal scholars condemned the introduction of "sociological and psychological evidences."[54] One critic Edmund Cahn judged the doll study to be logically weak and confusing. Historian Diane Ravitch agreed with these objections a generation later, posing herself as illogical question: "If segregated education is unconstitutional because social scientists say that causes psychological harm to children what happens if new sociological evidence emerges in the future to support a different finding?"[55]

The U.S. Supreme Court agreed with the Clarks. Chief Justice Earl Warren would cite the doll study in the majority opinion as the cornerstone of the Court's decision:

Does segregation of children in public schools solely on the basis of race ... deprive the children of minority groups of equal educational opportunities? We believe that it does. ...

Whatever may have been the extent of psychological knowledge at the time of *Plessy v. Ferguson*—this finding (by the Kansas Court in *Brown* that segregation denotes inferiority and diminishes learning motivation) is amply supported by modern authority. Any language in *Plessy v. Ferguson* is rejected.[56]

Bolstering his case, Warren included this forementioned, celebrated eleventh footnote citing the doll study. Historian of the *Brown* decision Richard Kluger would remark that the eleventh footnote "was to become one of the most debated in the analysis of the court."[57]

In 1987, the doll study was replicated. Dr. Darlene Powell Hopson and Sharon McNicoll conducted their studies in the United States and Trinidad. Their results confirmed the Clarks' original study. In the United States, 155 boys and girls were tested in Head Start preschool programs in New York City, Long Island, and Connecticut. Two-thirds of the students were asked which doll they would like to be, which was the "nice" doll, which was bad or nice, and which they preferred to own. The dolls were identical Cabbage Patch dolls except for color. Two-thirds of the black children preferred the white dolls. In Trinidad, 85 percent of the light-skinned children and 65 percent of the dark-skinned children opted for the white dolls.[58] Reviewing the replication study, Kenneth Clark found the results "disturbing" and warned that the psychological damage "will continue as long as racism continues."[59] The authors recommended a series of proposals to offset racism, chief of which was the establishment of an Afrocentric curriculum in the schools.

The doll study replication was criticized. Sociologist Judith Porter responded to the new study by stating that "she would hesitate to make claims about black children."[60] She cited "other research with black elementary and high school students" that "suggests that there has been an improvement in their racial self-esteem since the Clarks first did their studies."[61] It is a cruel commentary on the impact of the Civil Rights Movement and the persistence of racism that nearly thirty years later the self-esteem of black children remains low.

Moreover, the fragile nature of the psychology of black students has taken a dramatic turn. Somewhat due to the impact of the Black Power movement, which emphasized black pride and group cohesiveness, some black students deliberately abandon efforts to succeed academically for fear of "acting white." Anthropologists Signithia Fordham and John Ogbu conducted a study in 1986 that found that "in some segments of the black community there is a kind of cultural orientation which defines academic learning in school as 'acting white' and academic success the prerogative of white Americans."[62] According to these scholars, these black students "avoid adopting attitudes and putting enough time and effort in their school work because their peers (and themselves) would interpret their behavior as 'acting white.' "[63] They found a high correlation between poverty and such students.

Fordham and Ogbu collected their research at a Washington, D.C., high school that was 99 percent black and mostly poor. They conducted a case study, interviewing a cross-section of students, both high and low achievers. What they discovered was a pervasive black culture that stressed "group loyalty" and defined "certain attitudes and behaviors as 'white' and therefore unacceptable."[64] Included among these behaviors were such items as speaking standard English, studying hard for good grades, attending a symphony or listening to classical music, reading and writing poetry, and attending museums. Black students who were identified with these "behaviors" were derogatorily referred to as "brainiacs" and classified as "not truly black."[65]

Fordham and Obgu concluded that the fear of "acting white" is but an internalization of white racist views that perceived black intellectual achievement to be low. They argued that "because white Americans traditionally refused to acknowledge that black Americans are capable of intellectual achievement, and partly because black Americans subsequently began to doubt their own intellectual ability, and began to define academic success as white people's prerogative, and began to discourage their peers, perhaps unconsciously, from emulating white people in academic striving, i.e., from 'acting white.' "[66]

SOCIAL SCIENCE AND DESEGREGATION

The U.S. Supreme Court in *Brown* failed to set a specific deadline for public school desegregation. Rather, the Court offered the vague resolution that desegregation should proceed "with all deliberate speed."[67] Moreover, the Court entrusted desegregation to the localities, a decision that delayed school integration for at least a decade in many sections of the country as lower court challenges were decided. Research that showed the positive benefits of school integration, therefore, was eagerly received by civil rights leaders to prove their case.

The most important of these was the 1966 U.S. Office of Education's massive study by James Coleman and others, *Equality of Educational Opportunity*, more commonly referred to as the (first) Coleman Report. The study, named after the sociologist and chief researcher from Johns Hopkins University James Coleman, was authorized by the Civil Rights Act of 1964. It constituted the second largest social science study, after Gunnar Myrdal's on race in America, with some 645,000 public school students surveyed. The Coleman Report was a cross-sectional survey using an input-output quantitative methodology that, ironically, assessed a highly qualitative process—namely, learning. Coleman and his associates concluded that of all the quantitative variables—such as teachers' salaries, experience, and school resources—the most salient was family background. In short, what the child brings to the school, not what impact the school has on the child, was perceived as the most important.

There were ambiguities in the Coleman study. One was the finding that despite family background, poor black students in integrated classrooms performed well academically. Actually, the key variable was socioeconomic mix. Poor black or white students when integrated with the opposite black or white middle-class students performed well academically. Since there were more black poor than white poor to be integrated with black middle-class students, the Coleman Report was interpreted by civil rights leaders as a strong brief for school integration. Indeed, the next year the U.S. Civil Rights Commission would rework the Coleman Report to propose specific guidelines for congressional action on school desegregation. In their study, *Racial Isolation in the Public Schools*, the commission settled on a fifty-fifty ratio for mandated school desegregation. The measure failed in Congress.

Others amassed contrary evidence that school integration did not improve academic performance of blacks. Chief among these critics was David Armor whose 1972 study of school busing for integration in the Boston area challenged the research of such as Coleman's. In the Boston METCO program, Armor felt that he "was not able to demonstrate conclusively that integration had an effect on academic achievement as measured by standardized tests."[68] Armor found that there "were no increases in educational or occupational levels for bused students."[69] However, he hedged and admitted that researchers might have to "consider possible longer-term changes" since "no busing program had been in operation for more than seven years."[70]

Since that time, studies on the educational impact of school desegregation have been mixed. In a meta-analysis of 129 of these studies (a sophisticated quantitative review of the literature to establish trends), Ronald A. Kerol concluded that there was a "slightly positive" effect of desegregation on black students' school performance.[71] Robert L. Crain and Rita E. Mafard reviewed a number of studies and argued that "the evidence suggests" there is a "significant correlation between mandatory assignment and positive achievement outcomes."[72]

Ironically, nearly a decade after his report, Coleman would deliver a near fatal blow to school desegregation research. In a paper to the American Educational Research Association, Coleman presented "evidence" that school desegregation caused "white flight" from large cities to affluent suburbs, thus creating greater urban segregation. "Their flight from integration," Coleman argued, "appears to be principally a large-city phenomena."[73] Coleman thus handed opponents of desegregation a strong argument. Coleman's research was immediately denounced by civil rights leaders and liberals. In their analysis of the Coleman data, they challenged his conclusions. Coleman admitted that his interpretation may have gone "somewhat beyond the data."[74] Some scholars reviewing the Coleman data, such as Diane Ravitch, agreed with Coleman. Other scholars examined data from other cities and maintained "little or no 'white flight' " took place.[75] In her review of eighty-five school districts including such mega-cities as Boston, Denver, San Francisco, and Los Angeles, sociologist Christine Rossell declared that "it is impossible to contend that court-ordered racial assignment does accelerate 'white flight' in large cities."[76]

Nevertheless, the "white flight" theory gained ascendancy with critics of school desegregation, culminating in the Norfolk, Virginia, case in

which the U.S. Supreme Court ended mandatory busing for racial purposes. However, there are innumerable variables associated with "white
flight" that cannot be wholly attributable to public school desegregation.
The middle-class exodus to the suburbs that began after World War II
was partly a result of federal policies to build roads outward from the
cities and also a result of programs offering low-cost housing mortgage
loans to veterans and the general populace. With the building of high-
ways and suburban developments, the introduction of installment buy-
ing for automobiles followed suit. The United States was transformed
from an urban society into a suburban one. The migration to the suburbs
preceded "white flight" due to school desegregation, although the latter
may have in certain instances had some effect on the migration to the
suburbs.

In recent years the trek to the suburbs has been accompanied by "black
flight." African-American sociologist William Julius Wilson noted a substantial increase in the outmigration of middle-class blacks to the suburbs. Between 1970 and 1977 some 653,000 middle-class blacks left the
cities.[77] For Wilson, this migration has a downside: the weakening of the
socioeconomic infrastructure of urban ghettoes and the increase of poverty, crime, and hopelessness in those neighborhoods. Wilson argued
that "the exodus of middle- and working-class families from any ghetto
neighborhoods removes an important 'social buffer.' . . . [T]he very presence of these families during such periods provides mainstream role
models that help keep alive the perception that education is meaningful,
that steady employment is a viable alternative to welfare, and that family
stability is the norm, not the exception."[78]

THE NORFOLK CASE

A crucial turning point in the struggle to desegregate public schools
was the Norfolk, Virginia, case in 1986. City leaders and the school board
sought to dismantle cross-town busing for racial purposes. It became the
first major case to use the "white flight" argument.

Norfolk only began to desegregate its public schools in the 1969–1970
school years under court orders. At the time, 57 percent of the 56,830
public school students were white and 43 percent were black. With the
expansion of newly developed adjoining suburbs, the school population
declined to 34,803 students by 1983. The school system now had a black
majority of 58 percent and a white minority of 42 percent.[79] Moreover,
Norfolk's total population declined from 304,000 to 267,000 between 1960
and 1980.[80]

Citing "white flight," the Norfolk majority white school board voted
to abolish mandatory cross-town busing. The board proposed a neighborhood school plan that was challenged by civil rights activists in the

U.S. District Court. The court ruled in favor of the Norfolk school board, arguing that: "The Norfolk School Board is an integrated body, the school administration is racially balanced, the racial composition of faculty and staff is mixed and the overwhelming majority of school children, of both races, at the elementary, junior and senior high levels attend schools whose bodies are racially mixed. In addition, there has been no contention that extracurricular activities, transportation network, and school facilities are operated in a racially dual fashion."[81]

On appeal, the U.S. Court of Appeals for the Fourth Circuit agreed with the lower court's decision. The Court of Appeals concluded that Norfolk's plan was a "reasonable attempt by the school board to keep as many white students in public education as possible and to achieve a stable integrated school system."[82] In short, the jurists had accepted the "white flight" theory.

Two scholars from Old Dominion University analyzed the impact of the courts' decisions. Challenging school board consultant David Armor's prediction of a 7 percent annual return of white students with the dismantling of busing, Leslie G. Carr and Donald J. Ziegler found only an initial rate of 1 percent return for the first three years of their study and a fraction of a percent (.3%), in the fourth year—a meager gain of twenty-four white students.[83] They concluded that "factors other than busing for integration must be important to white parents."[84] Proceeding further, these scholars surveyed parents of both black and white public school students. Their survey indicated a large racial divide between the two. Fully three-fourths of white parents approved of the neighborhood school plan, whereas a similar percentage of black parents disapproved.[85]

Most important, the Norfolk school system became resegregated. The number of schools with a 75 percent black enrollment tripled, and the number of segregated schools rose from 17 percent in 1985 to 39 percent in 1989.[86] They concluded that the courts had mistakenly based their decisions on the "erroneous argument" of "white flight."[87] Moreover, scholar Vivian Ikpa, analyzing the Norfolk data, added that in 1992 both black and white students in third and fourth grades were to "experience declines in test scores after the elimination of the policy of mandated busing."[88]

DESEGREGATION FORTY YEARS LATER

The height of the desegregation movement in public schools was 1976, at which point there was a 50 percent decrease in segregated schools.[89] Most of this change took place *de jure* in southern schools, whereas *de facto* segregation in northern cities worsened.

A 1993 study, Harvard University's Project on School Desegregation, revealed that minority students were more segregated than at any time since the late 1960s. The report indicated that 66 percent of black students attended predominantly minority schools, defined as having 50 percent or more minority students.[90] In addition, 74.3 percent of Hispanic students attended predominantly minority schools.[91]

In the early 1990s, Jonathan Kozol toured a number of cities for an in-depth investigation. Kozol visited East St. Louis, Illinois; Chicago; New York City; Camden, New Jersey; Washington, D.C.; and San Antonio, Texas. He found schools that were 95 to 99 percent black in neighborhoods "where every face is black, where there were simply no white people anywhere."[92] He was startled by "the remarkable degree of racial segregation that persisted almost everywhere."[93] For Kozol "the nation, for all practical purposes and intent, has turned its back upon the moral implications, if not yet, the legal ramifications of the *Brown* decision."[94]

Compounding this racial isolation is crippling poverty. As of 1993, nearly half of black children under 18 were living in poverty, mostly in cities.[95] Three decades of educational research have linked poor school performance with poverty. Moreover, as Kozol detailed in *Savage Inequalities*, these poorest neighborhoods receive the smallest amount of funds for their schools due to a system based largely on local property taxes. Nor has the poverty of African Americans as a whole substantially improved. In 1960, 31 percent of the black population was identified as poor; thirty years later that percentage would minimally decrease to 29 percent.[96] For African-American historian Manning Marable, school desegregation has aided middle-class blacks but few poor ones. Marable declared that desegregation "without the transfer of [economic] power to blacks as a racial group" has left much to be desired.[97]

What has also happened to school desegregation is a demographic change. With the migration of middle-class blacks and Hispanics to the suburbs and the increase of urban *de facto* segregation, Gary Orfield saw the need for "greater attention to issues of suburban desegregation."[98]

THE EQUITY REFORM MOVEMENT

The black struggle for equality triggered a larger educational reform movement. It energized a cadre of mostly white educational reformers who offered a wide range of solutions to American education. The key was poverty and the need for social mobility through the schools.

Dovetailing with the Civil Rights Movement was an influential critique of U.S. society written by a young socialist who had been immersed in Catholic social action. Michael Harrington's *The Other America*, published in 1962, detailed the "invisible poor" who existed in an otherwise affluent society. Since much of the poverty in the United States was black poverty, Harrington's critique complemented the efforts of civil rights activists (Harrington was to become an advisor to Rev. Martin Luther

King, Jr.). Harrington's book was read by President John F. Kennedy and set the stage for President Lyndon Johnson's war on poverty, a crucial element of which was education. Interestingly, Harrington neglected to mention education in his book. Rather, he considered housing as "perhaps the most crucial element in racial poverty."[99] Nevertheless, Johnson, a former school teacher, was adamant that the federal government's social programs were to emphasize education.

Harrington was optimistic about eliminating poverty. "The means are at hand to fulfill an age old dream," he urged; "poverty can now be abolished."[100] By the 1980s, he would revise that statement as world economies challenged that of the United States. "The great, impersonal forces have indeed created a context," he reflected, "in which poverty is much more difficult to abolish than it was twenty-five years ago."[101]

The educational reformers of the equity movement shared the same romantic concept of the poor as did their progressive forbears. For these reformers the poor were in a state of grace, especially school children, later to be brutalized by outside economic conditions. The educational literature attested to this romantic perception. Nat Hentoff's portrait of urban schooling was entitled *Our Children Are Dying*; Paul Goodman's was called *Growing Up Absurd*; and Jonathan Kozol's was accusingly titled *Death at an Early Age: The Destruction of the Hearts and Minds of Negro Children in the Boston Public Schools*. For these romantic educational reformers, the system was to blame. Characteristically Kozol pictured the ghetto school's effect on black children "in terms you cannot avoid recognizing, the dreadful consequences of a year's wastage of real lives."[102]

The equity reform movement was geared to educating the poor. Diane Ravitch characterized the movement as the emergence of a "new consensus" that "was founded on the belief in the failure of the schools."[103] Educational solutions proposed by these romantic reformers created a mosaic of exciting educational ideas. Indeed, there were so many ideas that Ravitch noted: "Every new idea had a constituency, whether it was racial balancing of schools, parent participation, black community control, or anything else that promised to break the grip of traditional practice."[104]

Ravitch correctly assessed that for these romantic reformers innovation was prized over existing practices, "that the only change worth attempting must be of a fundamental, institutional systemic kind," and that "there was little in the schools worth preserving."[105] (Indeed, I often heard my colleague Marilyn Gittell, a major actor in the community control movement, condemn incremental reform and argue for systemwide change.) For Ravitch, these views of educational change were wrongly directed. Ironically, Ravitch would become a key player in the excellence reform movement of the 1980s, even serving as an education aide to President George Bush. As an excellence reformer, she advocated the need for innovation and fundamental change (to the point of recommending federal vouchers for school children to attend private schools) that she condemned in the equity school reformers.

A national agenda for school reform was set by President Johnson. Inheriting the agenda of his predecessor, Johnson would focus educational reform on poverty. Although the federal government never accounted for more than 9 percent of the nation's educational costs (a high reach during the Johnson administration), its choice of educational programs established the pattern for the states and localities to follow. The equity reform movement, then, was an attempt to successfully educate the nation's poor. The movement dominated American education for two decades until the counterexcellence reform movement of the 1980s. The excellence reform movement sought to educate the other end of the spectrum—the best and the brightest—in order to compete economically in the global marketplace.

Johnson's Great Society programs offered, according to U.S. Commissioner of Education Harold Howe II, "change money" that sought "institutional change, curricula change, organizational change" so as "to meet the problems of modern America."[106] The two most celebrated Great Society initiatives were the historic 1965 Elementary and Secondary Education Act that funded innovation programs for the poor in the elementary schools and the Head Start program for preschooling for the poor. Early studies noted that these programs were initially ineffective due to problems of implementation. Later longitudinal studies were more positive.[107] By the early 1990s, however, renewed attacks on these programs once again criticized their implementation.[108] Interestingly, the founder of Head Start, Edward Zigler, responding to this criticism, invoked the rhetoric of the progressives. Head Start, he declared, "has focused on the whole child."[109] By that he meant dental and social services rather than the intellectual, moral, artistic, and social aims of the progressives. The new progressives would employ the language of the original progressives but with altered meanings.

AFFIRMATIVE ACTION

In June 1965, President Johnson proclaimed his boldest plan for obtaining civil rights in the United States. In a speech entitled "To Fulfill These Rights," given at Howard University, Johnson declared that the nation must move beyond "legal equity" toward "equality as a fact and equality as a result."[110] Thus, Johnson made a significant shift in government policy from providing equality of opportunity to equality of results.

The first fleshing out of this new policy of equality of results was affirmative action. Johnson declared Executive Order 11246 that would pursue a policy in education and employment where schools and businesses must give preferential treatment to minorities and women in admissions and jobs when faced with equally qualified candidates. For over a generation, affirmative action has proved a most divisive policy.

The underlying rationale behind affirmative action is simple. For the past three hundred years, majority America has held back the progress of African Americans (and other minorities in varying measure) first through slavery and later through racial discrimination. In order to make up for past injustices and to hasten the social mobility of these groups, affirmative action calls for preferential treatment. The U.S. Supreme Court has upheld the principle of affirmative action while deciding on the merits of specific plans.

Critics have charged "reverse racism." Sociologist Nathan Glazer in his book *Affirmative Discrimination* criticized affirmative action from moving toward a "color-blind" society, purportedly attained by the Civil Rights Movement, to a "color—and group—consciousness with a vengeance."[111] For Glazer, "public policy must be exercised without distinction of race, color, or national origin."[112] Glazer was sympathetic to the white ethnic backlash to affirmative action. He challenged the "moral advantage" of affirmative action, which "is not everything, it is important to consider how the American political system works."[113]

Glazer's crucial assumption was that racial discrimination had been substantially eliminated. Commenting on the Civil Rights Movement, Glazer declared that "Negro progress during this period was indeed marked," thus not necessitating affirmative action.[114] However, by the early 1990s, the evidence failed to support this view. William Julius Wilson, whose earlier study *The Declining Significance of Race* agreed with Glazer, discovered new data that indicated otherwise: namely, that racial discrimination was still firmly embedded in American society. In the Urban and Poverty Family Life Study in Chicago, Wilson and his colleagues collected data from 2,500 blacks and Hispanics in neighborhoods that were at least 20 percent below the poverty line. Employers hired blacks last, preferring Hispanics. These employers believed that blacks did not want to work, and they were fearful of potential crime. His research led Wilson to conclude that "it becomes clear that racism is far more important than I once believed."[115]

CONCLUSION

The equity reform movement diminished as the Civil Rights Movement, which largely created it, also declined. The decline of the Civil Rights Movement in the 1970s and 1980s was due to a number of factors. First, the movement largely succeeded in two of three main objectives: gaining access to areas of American life that had been closed due largely to institutional racism, and enabling African Americans to be elected to public office. The one area that proved most intractable was economic. Civil rights leaders were not able to resolve the economic dilemma of fully one-third of the black community who remained in poverty. Externally, the Civil Rights Movement was victim of strong national backlash. After 1968, conservative Republican Party rule was not beholden to a black constituency firmly rooted in the Democratic Party. The reaction to the social innovation of the 1960s and the confrontational tactics that brought it about invigorated a dormant ultra-conservatism that reached its apex with the election of President Ronald Reagan in 1980.

As the influence of the Civil Rights Movement waned, so did that of the romantic educational reformers. Without a strong constituency to press for educational change, educational policy was at a stasis. Consequently, the shift from equity to excellence reform in the 1980s was accomplished with minimum difficulty.

Nonetheless, the romantic reformers and civil rights leaders made great strides and changed education in the United States. Their focus on the education of the poor surpassed the efforts of the progressives. The reformers were able to accelerate the development of educational research, mostly focused on the education of the poor. Thus, they were able to pursue a high moral agenda with dedication and reasonable success.

However, the equity reform movement raised a large question still to be answered. With the passing of the influence of progressive education by the 1950s, American education lacked a coherent, viable educational philosophy. The romantic reformers were unable to fill the philosophical gap. We have had no new John Deweys to chart a direction. This fact was made painfully clear in my involvement with the community control movement. In his report to the community-controlled school board in Harlem in 1969, African-American administrator Charles Wilson complained of the "confusion about an overall philosophy or master plan for educational change."[116] The investigations of Marilyn Gittell, myself, and the other staff members of the Institute for Community Studies led us to conclude that "One cannot fault the demonstration districts for their lack of educational philosophy. The same is true of most educators and school systems throughout the country."[117] Neither was the excellence reform movement able to generate a holistic new educational philosophy unique to American society.

NOTES

1. Diane Ravitch, *The Troubled Crusade: American Education 1945–1980* (New York: Basic Books, 1983), p. 255.

2. Meyer Weinberg, "The Civil Rights Movement and Educational Change,"

in *The Education of African-Americans,* edited by Charles V. Willie, Antoine M. Earibalds, and Wornie L. Reed (New York: Auburn House, 1991), p. 3.

3. Francis Keppel, "Thank God for the Civil Rights Movement," *Integrated Education,* vol. 3, April/May 1964, pp. 9–10.

4. Preston R. Wilcox, "The Community-Centered School," in *The Schoolhouse in the City,* edited by Alvin Toffler (New York: Praeger, 1968), pp. 99–100.

5. W.E.B. DuBois, *The Autobiography of W.E.B. DuBois* (New York: International Publishers, 1968), p. 102.

6. *Ibid.,* p. 133.

7. *Ibid.,* p. 143.

8. *Ibid.,* p. 248.

9. *Ibid.,* p. 236.

10. W.E.B. DuBois, "Does the Negro Need Separate Schools?" *Journal of Negro Education,* July 1935, pp. 328–329.

11. *Ibid.,* p. 329.

12. *Ibid.,* p. 333.

13. *Ibid.,* p. 330.

14. *Ibid.,* p. 335.

15. W.E.B. DuBois, *The Education of Black People: Ten Critiques 1906–1960* (Amherst: University of Massachusetts Press, 1973), p. 151.

16. *Ibid.*

17. *Ibid.*

18. *Ibid.*

19. David J. Garrow, *Bearing the Cross: Martin Luther King, Jr., and the Southern Christian Leadership Conference* (New York: William Morrow and Co., 1986), p. 37.

20. *Ibid.,* p. 38.

21. *Ibid.*

22. Martin Luther King, Jr., *Whether Do We Go From Here?* (New York: Harper & Row, 1967), p. 193.

23. *Ibid.*

24. *Ibid.,* p. 195.

25. *Ibid.,* pp. 194–195.

26. *Ibid.,* pp. 44, 199.

27. *Ibid.,* p. 44.

28. *Ibid.,* p. 162.

29. Joseph Carpenter, Jr., *The Leadership Philosophy of Dr. Martin Luther King, Jr.: Its Educational Implications,* Ph.D. dissertation (Ann Arbor: University of Michigan, 1971), p. 168.

30. *Ibid.,* p. 147.

31. *Ibid.,* p. 161.

32. Alex Haley, *The Autobiography of Malcolm X* (New York: Ballantine Books Edition, February 1992), p. 35.

33. *Ibid.,* p. 37.

34. *Ibid.*

35. *Ibid.,* p. 437.

36. *Ibid.*

37. *Ibid.,* p. 335.

38. *Ibid.,* p. 199.

39. *Ibid.*, p. 207.

40. Malcolm X, *February 1965: The Final Speeches* (New York: Pathfinder Press, 1992), p. 39.

41. *Ibid.*, p. 60.

42. *Ibid.*

43. *Ibid.*, p. 261.

44. *Ibid.*

45. Charles V. Willie, "The Future of School Desegregation," in *The Education of African-Americans*, edited by Charles V. Willie et al. (New York: Auburn House, 1991), p. 52.

46. Robert A. Dentler, "School Desegregation Since Gunnar Myrdal's *American Dilemma*," in *The Education of African-Americans*, edited by Charles V. Willie et al. (New York: Auburn House, 1991), p. 46.

47. David J. Armor, "The Evidence on Busing," *The Public Interest*, Summer 1972.

48. Ravitch, *The Troubled Crusade*, p. 127.

49. Richard Kluger, *Simple Justice: The History of Brown v. Board of Education and Black America's Struggle for Equality* (New York: Alfred A. Knopf, 1976), p. 256.

50. Ravitch, *The Troubled Crusade*, p. 121.

51. Kluger, *Simple Justice*, p. 294.

52. *Ibid.*, p. 318.

53. *Ibid.*

54. Ravitch, *The Troubled Crusade*, p. 129.

55. *Ibid.*, p. 130.

56. Kluger, *Simple Justice*, pp. 704–705.

57. *Ibid.*, p. 705.

58. *New York Times*, August 31, 1987, p. A9.

59. *Ibid.*

60. *Ibid.*

61. *Ibid.*

62. *New York Times*, April 25, 1990, p. B9.

63. *Ibid.*

64. Signithia Fordham and John U. Ogbu, "Black Students' School Success: Coping with the 'Burden of Acting White,' " *The Urban Review*, vol. 18, no. 3, 1986, p. 185.

65. *Ibid.*, p. 188.

66. *Ibid.*, p. 177.

67. Dentler, "School Desegregation," p. 31.

68. Armor, "The Evidence on Busing," p. 99.

69. *Ibid.*, p. 101.

70. *Ibid.*, p. 105.

71. Meyer Weinberg, *The Search for Quality Integrated Education* (Westport, Conn.: Greenwood Press, 1983), p. 150.

72. *Ibid.*

73. Diane Ravitch, "The 'White Flight' Controversy," *The Public Interest*, Spring 1978, p. 136.

74. *Ibid.*

75. *Ibid.*, p. 137.

76. *Ibid.*

77. William Julius Wilson, *The Truly Disadvantaged* (Chicago: The University of Chicago Press, 1987), p. 34.

78. *Ibid.*, p 56.

79. Thomas J. Flygare, "A Return to Neighborhood Schools as a Way of Stemming 'White Flight,' " *Phi Delta Kappan*, May 1986, p. 679.

80. Leslie G. Carr and Donald J. Ziegler, "White Flight and White Return in Norfolk: A Test of Predictions," *Sociology of Education*, vol. 63, 1990, p. 273.

81. Flygare, "A Return to Neighborhood Schools," p. 679.

82. *Ibid.*, p. 680.

83. Carr and Ziegler, "White Flight and White Return," p. 279.

84. *Ibid.*

85. *Ibid.*, p. 280.

86. *Ibid.*, p. 281.

87. *Ibid.*

88. Vivian Ikpa, "Gender Race, Chapter I Participation: The Effects of Individual Characteristics Upon Academic Performance in the Elementary Grades," *Educational Research Quarterly*, vol. 16, no. 1, 1992, p. 18.

89. Willie, "The Future of School Desegregation," p. 52.

90. *New York Times*, December 14, 1993, p. 1.

91. *Ibid.*

92. Jonathan Kozol, *Savage Inequalities* (New York: Crown Publishers, 1991), p. 3.

93. *Ibid.*, p. 4.

94. *Ibid.*

95. *New York Times*, October 5, 1993, p. A20.

96. *Virginian Ledger-Star*, August 27, 1993, p. A2.

97. Manning Marable, *Race, Reform and Rebellion: The Second Reconstruction in Black America, 1945–1990* (Jackson: University Press of Mississippi, 1991), p. 190.

98. Gary Orfield and Franklin Monfort et al., *Status of School Desegregation: The Next Generation* (Cambridge, Mass.: Harvard University Metropolitan Opportunity Project, January 8, 1992), p. 4.

99. Michael Harrington, *The Other America: Poverty in the United States* (New York: The Macmillan Co., 1962), p. 79.

100. *Ibid.*, p. 174.

101. Michael Harrington, *The New American Poverty* (New York: Holt, Rinehart and Winston, 1984), p. 2.

102. Jonathan Kozol, *Death at an Early Age: The Destruction of the Hearts and Minds of Negro Children in the Boston Public Schools* (Boston: Houghton Mifflin, 1967), p. 185.

103. Ravitch, *The Troubled Crusade*, p. 237.

104. *Ibid.*

105. *Ibid.*, pp. 237–238.

106. Harold Howe II, "Oral History Interview," transcript, Austin, Tex.: Lyndon Baines Johnson Presidential Library, July 12, 1968, p. 8.

107. Irving Lazar and Richard B. Darlington, *Lasting Effects After Preschool* (Ithaca, N.Y.: Cornell University, October 1978); John R. Berrueta-Clement et al.,

Changed Lives: The Effects of the Perry Preschool Program on Youths Through Age 19 (Ypsilanti, Mich.: High/Scope Press, 1984).

108. *New York Times*, February 23, 1993, p. A16.

109. Edward Zigler, "Head Start, The Whole Story," *New York Times*, July 24, 1993, p. 19.

110. Lyndon B. Johnson, "To Fulfill These Rights," in *The Great Society Reader*, edited by Marvin Gettleman and David Mermelstein (New York: Random House, 1967), p. 254.

111. Nathan Glazer, *Affirmative Discrimination* (New York: Basic Books, 1975), p. 3.

112. *Ibid.*, p. 221.

113. *Ibid.*, p. 210.

114. *Ibid.*, p. 41.

115. Gretchen Reynolds, "The Rising Significance of Race," *Chicago*, December 1992, p. 128.

116. Marilyn Gittell with Maurice R. Berube et al., *Local Control in Education: Three Demonstration School Districts in New York City* (New York: Praeger, 1972), p. 98.

117. *Ibid.*, p. 99.

CHAPTER FIVE

COMMUNITY CONTROL REVISITED

The Civil Rights Movement would have another direct impact on the direction of American education. With the shift from an emphasis on school integration to Black Power, African-American educational activists sought a measure of control over the operation of schools. This phenomenon, called community control, emerged in cities with large numbers of black poor, most notably in New York City. Community control would leave a lasting imprint on the face of urban education and the schooling of African Americans and other minorities.

PARTICIPATION

In the 1960s, the key social concept was that of participation. Spurred by the Civil Rights Movement, a number of social activists argued for expanding the fabric of our democratic society to include those who had been traditionally bypassed, namely, the poor. The idea of expanding participation in the political, social, and institutional life of Americans to the poor was essentially reformist. However, it was perceived by critics as a radical and threatening proposal. Civil rights leader Stokely Carmichael (Kwame Ture) commented twenty-six years after he proclaimed the doctrine of Black Power that he was "greeted [with a] great deal of hostility," which he found "surprising" since he did not "advocate Revolution."[1]

The scholarly basis for expanding political participation to the poor rested with the work of Richard Cloward and Lloyd Ohlin. The two sociologists worked with juvenile delinquents in New York City and discovered that the sense of alienation associated with lower income groups was dispelled when these youngsters felt some control over their lives through participation. Social scientists of that time concluded that the poor did not want to participate in political activities. They were not apt to vote in political elections nor become involved in community or school activities. Cloward and Ohlin's work suggested otherwise—that, in fact, when presented with opportunities for meaningful participation, the poor were no longer alienated.

Certainly, the Civil Rights Movement was a clear example of this thesis. More important, the Civil Rights Movement clearly influenced the popularity of that idea in the liberal community. In 1962, the young, New Left radicals of Students for a Democratic Society (SDS) would strike the theme of "participatory democracy." Two years later, the federal administration would have the credo in the poverty program of "maximum feasible participation of the residents of the areas."[2] And two years after that, Stokely Carmichael's cry for Black Power was but another instance of the idea of participation. Black Power was no less that African Americans obtaining a determining voice in those institutions that governed their lives. One of the first embodiments of Black Power proved to be community control in urban public schools.

In its 1962 Port Huron statement, written by activists Tom Hayden and Al Haber, SDS would proclaim that "as a social system we seek the establishment of a democracy of individual participation . . . that the individual share in those social decisions determining the quality and direction of his life."[3] According to one historian of SDS, the 61-page document, 100,000 copies of which were distributed, "launched SDS as a national movement."[4] The radical New Left was born.

Stokely Carmichael would further the participation theme. He wrote in *Black Power*, along with Charles Hamilton, "Black Power therefore calls for black people to consolidate beyond their own so that they can bargain from a position of strength."[5] Most important, he argued that "Black Power—is full participation in the decision-making processes affecting the lives of black people."[6]

It was but a short step from Black Power to community control. Columbia professor Preston R. Wilcox, the African-American theorist of the community control movement, wrote that what was needed in public schools was a "community presence [so that] an instrumentality be developed which assures minority group parents of direct access to the channels of informed opinion and power."[7] For Wilcox, "the communities of the poor must be prepared to act for themselves."[8] Carmichael endorsed Wilcox's version of Black Power: "We must begin to think of the black community as a base of organization to control institutions in that community. Control of the ghetto schools must be taken out of the hands of the professionals. . . . [T]he concept of community control has rooted itself in the consciousness of black people."[9]

Some considered that the early Civil Rights Movement had set the stage for the drive for black political participation. The confrontational methods of Rev. Martin Luther King, Jr., and his associates, in the marches and boycotts in the South, were a "politics of protest and confrontation" that signalled the need for change in city, state, and federal government. A high-level aide to New York Mayor John Lindsay, Frederick O. Hayes would argue to his cabinet colleagues that "participation of the poor was not an option—but a necessity" since "the civil rights movement was in full flower . . . [and] a new day was already at hand, and it had best been recognized if the urban poor were to cooperate with us in their own betterment."[10] The latter suggestion had a paternalistic ring. Nevertheless the idea that participation had a strong push from the Civil Rights Movements has much merit.

The essence of community control in education was simple. School boards in the various urban communities would be elected by parents with children in the public schools. This idea originated with Wilcox and the Harlem school activists to ensure proper representation. These boards would have meaningful power: over school policy—namely, over personnel, curriculum, and finance. Prior to the community control movement, most urban school boards were appointed rather than elected. On the other hand, suburban boards were, for the most part, elected. The difference was the direct result of the progressives replacing corrupt, ethnic politics in cities with a more professional arrangement based on civil service examinations. However, the demographics had changed whereby the suburbs became mostly white and affluent and the cities black and poor.

The reason that black activists demanded community control of public schools in urban ghettos was equally simple. For them, the schools had failed their children. Protests by civil rights groups had succeeded in getting city boards of education to release test scores for the first time. In Harlem, approximately 85 percent of school children were more than two years behind in reading. In one year about thirteen Harlem youngsters in Harlem's only high school received an academic diploma.[11] What was true of Harlem was true of most urban schools with large, poor black and Hispanic populations. In Washington, D.C., four out of five pupils were behind in reading.[12] Black activists concluded that the educational system did not work for their children. They argued that they could do no worse by running the schools themselves.

But community control posed a vexing question: Did America want school policy determined by an elected board of parents who were poor and probably undereducated? More important, these parents would be black, assertive, and possibly hostile to white society. For one nationally know journalist and former New York City appointed school board member, the answer was no. Martin Mayer would write of the Ocean

Hill–Brownsville school board, one of three experiments in community control, that the "elected parent representatives, all mothers and most on welfare," were "very ignorant."[13] For Mayer, "you have to know a hell of a lot before you can intelligently tell a superintendent of schools what to do."[14]

Other observers were more optimistic. They acknowledged the parents' political "right to participate in the educational process" despite "their lack initially of having the technical qualifications to make such a [policy] decision.[15] Naomi Levine and Richard Cohen argued that participation of ghetto parents might result in increased expertise "so their concerns broaden," and an "ever-freshening source of new energy, new ideas, and true partners in education might result."[16] An evaluation of the three experiments in community control proved this to be true. Written by Marilyn Gittell, myself, and others, the study entitled *Local Control in Education* indicated that both the expertise and the willingness to experiment educationally were characteristic of those boards.

The idea of elected school boards itself was not universally popular. Professor Charles Judd had maintained in the 1930s that all school boards should be eliminated and education policy be made by those he felt knew best, namely, teachers and administrators. But by the 1960s urban politics had changed the attitudes of parents. As one New York City mayoral aide conceded, "the strongest component of the participatory ideology was anti-professionalism, the need to arm the poor . . . against the teacher and the social worker."[17]

The critics of the participation ideology were many and crossed traditionally liberal/conservative lines. Prominent liberal Daniel P. Moynihan would rail against the concept and dedicate a book, *Maximum Feasible Misunderstanding*, to its denunciation. Moynihan argued that participation was no less than "social science at its very weakest, at its worst," since it offered a theory of "individual or collective behavior which raises the possibility, by controlling certain inputs, of bringing about mass behavioral change."[18] He warned that community control might improve school performance, "but then again, it might *not*."[19]

AFROCENTRISM

There was another large question raised by the community control movement. The experiments in community control first raised the issue of an Afrocentric curriculum in the public schools. From the first demonstration for community control in 1966, parents carried placards proclaiming that "Black Children Need Black Culture."[20] One African American, Karima Jordan, recalled her student days at the community control experiment junior high school in Ocean Hill–Brownsville as her first contact with black teachers and black culture: "What the black teachers did was to broaden us, our perspective of looking at things. . . . We were broadened to W.E.B. DuBois, his writings, Langston Hughes, Malcolm X, Marcus Garvey, H. Rap Brown, Mao Tse-tung, the Red Book. They brought us back to ancient African history. . . . We became much larger than just the community."[21]

However, resistance by whites to a multicultural curriculum was deep. It has not abated with the passage of time. However, African-American educators have continued to promote "the importance of an Afrocentric, multicultural curriculum."[22] In 1993, Kimberly R. Vann and Jawanza Kunjufu argued that "the experiences of all cultures involved must be equally recognized and legitimated" since "a strictly Eurocentric perspective will not properly prepare students for a successful future in a multicultural world."[23]

COMMUNITY CONTROL

The year 1966 marked a watershed in the Civil Rights Movement. The goal of racial integration was challenged by young African-American civil rights leaders. The concept of Black Power emerged. When James Meredith, the first African-American student to attend the University of Mississippi, was shot on his solo civil rights march, the setting was established for a reconstituted, massive civil rights march. It was on that march in June that Stokely Carmichael proclaimed the goal of Black Power. Rev. Martin Luther King, Jr., responded with maintaining the need for African Americans to seek integration. Black Power proved a highly controversial concept but slowly won in the end, with most African Americans accepting its main tenets.

That same spring a group of African-American activists in Harlem despaired of integrating public schools. They concluded that the New York City Board of Education had not sincerely sought to integrate the schools. Black children were failing in massive numbers. They reasoned that they could do no worse by running the schools themselves. Preston Wilcox proposed that a "School-Community Committee" be comprised of "parents, local leaders and professionals in education, or outside if necessary" to operate one particular school, newly built Intermediate School 201 on West 126th Street in Harlem.[24] Moreover, the school committee would be "selected by parents of children in the school."[25] A key demand was for a black male principal to serve as a role model for the students. Unfortunately, there were no such principals in the New York City system, and only 8 percent of the teachers were black in a system that enrolled a majority of minority students.[26] In order to obtain a principal's license, a candidate was determined qualified by a written civil service examination.

That fall, on opening day of school, the parents and civil rights leaders boycotted I.S. 201. They were later joined by national civil rights leaders such as Stokely Carmichael and Floyd McKissick, head of the Congress of Racial Equality (CORE). The central Board of Education acceded to the boycotters' demands. But the school teachers (including a black female assistant principal) counter-boycotted, and the agreement of the parental group was negated.

The I.S. 201 boycott triggered wider protests. A parental group in the Ocean Hill–Brownsville section of Brooklyn approached the teachers' union—the United Federation of Teachers (UFT), AFL-CIO—for support in their demands for parental involvement. At a January meeting of the central board, civil rights activists disrupted the public meeting and declared themselves a "People's Board of Education." They adopted a motion that would "seek to alter the structure of the school system . . . in order to achieve real community control."[27]

Alarmed at the growing unrest, Mayor John Lindsay sought to restructure the public schools toward increasing parental involvement. Since educational power resides with the states, Lindsay commissioned a blue ribbon panel to recommend to the state legislature changes in school governance. The panel was headed by McGeorge Bundy, president of the Ford Foundation. Key advisors to the panel included educator Mario Fantini, Bundy's aide at Ford, and political scientist Marilyn Gittell, a professor at Queens College. Gittell's earlier study *Participants and Participation* was a forerunner of the community control movement. The Bundy plan, entitled *Reconnection for Learning*, incorporated much of the demands of black activists for community control: school boards elected by parents with children in the public schools; substantial power over personnel, finance, and curriculum; alternate certification methods for the appointment of administrators.

However, before the Bundy plan was finally formulated, the mayor, along with State Commissioner of Education James Allen, took the initiative to establish experimental school boards in community control. Normal procedures in hiring administrators were bypassed allowing for the first minority administrators in the system. The three districts were I.S. 201 in Harlem; Ocean Hill–Brownsville in Brooklyn, recommended by the teachers' union; and Two Bridges on the Lower East Side, suggested by the Ford Foundation as a"melting pot." The I.S. 201 and Ocean Hill–Brownsville experiments, comprised of blacks and Hispanics, were successful, whereas the Two Bridges district, comprised of many ethnic groups, was virtually ineffective since the groups could not reach a consensus on most issues.

The experiments were embattled from the beginning. The teachers' union and the principals' association were early antagonists. UFT president Albert Shanker protested the appointment of African-American Rhody McCoy as unit administrator of the Ocean Hill experiment in a wild melee at a school board meeting that involved the throwing of chairs. McCoy had been an administrator in a school for disturbed children. Soft spoken and extremely cautious, McCoy was determined to represent his constituency. Many years later, it was learned that McCoy was influenced by Malcolm X and had visited him in his home many times to discuss educational goals for black children.[28] The principals' association leaders were upset that the normal civil service tests for administrators had been suspended for the experiments. They filed suit in the courts, challenging the legality of the procedures to select experimental community control superintendents and principals.

The key actor was Albert Shanker. An extremely bright and charismatic young union leader, Shanker had long considered himself a liberal. A socialist in college, he was to hire many of the socialist aides of civil rights leader Bayard Rustin for the UFT staff and later the national staff when he became president. Shanker had marched the last few laps with Rev. Martin Luther King, Jr., in Selma, Alabama, in 1965 in the drive for voting rights. He supported the union's policy of integration. At the outbreak of the I.S. 201 conflict, he initially advised the teachers at the school to support the parents. Thus, it was a cruel irony that he was to be accused of being one of the most prominent white racist demagogues in New York City's history. By 1991 African-American historian Manning Marable would characterize Shanker as a "racist social democrat" who fought to oppose "the installment of 'affirmative action' policies."[29]

Two factors changed Shanker's stance. First, he was quick to realize that community control would introduce a competing player in education. The union had won the nation's first collective bargaining agreement a few short years prior and was rapidly exerting its influence. Shanker argued that "decentralization has no educational relevance at all."[30] As a consummate union leader, he was intent on preserving the educational power of the teachers.

The episode proved traumatic for Shanker. Asked by *Newsweek* magazine in 1993 what "three changes would make schools better," Shanker called for the elimination of school boards altogether: "I'd find a substitute for school boards—basically, what we need to have is superintendents and principals who will let the professionals (teachers) do what works. We need to get the political interference with teachers off their backs."[31]

More important in the long run was the paternalistic racism of many northern liberals. Civil rights in the South was a cause northern liberals could espouse safely, but Black Power and civil rights in the North was another matter altogether. Reflecting on the confrontation in community control twenty-five years later, Sorbonne professor Sophie Body-Gendrot cited 1967–1968 as the time when "a crucial ideological change for a majority of the left" had occurred.[32]

CONFRONTATION

The inevitable clash occurred between the teachers' union and the Ocean Hill–Brownsville school board. The board submitted a list of thirteen teachers and assistant principals to be returned to the central board of education for transfer to other schools. Transfer was the standard operating procedure. These teachers had allegedly been undermining the experiment at Ocean Hill. According to UFT staffer Irving Weinstein, Shanker perceived the transfers as the opening to scuttle the experiments. He labeled the transfers as "firings" and therefore a violation of due process, although the union contract had scant provisions in this regard. Shanker led a series of three citywide strikes in the fall of 1968. Only the experimental school districts remained open. The New York Civil Liberties Union condemned the UFT for using " 'due process' as a smoke screen to obscure its real goal, which is to discredit decentralization and sabotage community control."[33] Martin Mayer called the confrontation between an overwhelmingly white—and largely Jewish—teachers' union and the black community "the worst disaster my native city has experienced in my lifetime."[34]

For the first time, the black leadership in the city closed ranks behind McCoy and the Ocean Hill governing board. The one exception was Bayard Rustin, whose A. Philip Randolph Institute was funded by the AFL-CIO and was housed in UFT headquarters. Consequently, it was not surprising that Rustin would be the 1968 recipient of the UFT's John Dewey Medal for outstanding leadership.

Support came from another source. Soon to be elected president of the United States, Richard Nixon offered his opinion a few days before the election that he did not "believe that any teacher has an obligation to work under the conditions I understand had prevailed in the Ocean Hill–Brownsville district."[35]

The turning point was the emergence of black anti-Semitism. In a city with a large Jewish population, many of whom were prominent in education and the press, black anti-Semitism had a devastating effect. A strain of black anti-Semitism has been prevalent to this day, from the 1984 presidential campaign by Jesse Jackson referring to New York City as "Hymietown" or Louis Farrakhan's reference to Judaism as a "dirty religion" to the black rap group Public Enemy's denigrating remarks about Jews. On the other side of the ledger, there had existed within some elements of the Jewish community a strain of racism that first revealed itself in the Ocean Hill conflict and later in such disputes as Forest Hill's New York housing controversy over scatter site housing, introducing public housing for poor blacks in a largely middle-class Jewish community.

The precipitating incident was the distribution by an unknown person of a few anti-Semitic leaflets in the teachers' mailboxes in Ocean Hill. At this point, the reaction was clear: Albert Shanker and the UFT had a half million reprints of the leaflets run off and distributed throughout the city at subway stops, supermarkets, and street corners. The end result was, in American Federation of Teachers (AFT) president David Selden's analysis, that "the leaflet united the city's Jewish population behind the UFT."[36] Shanker would further escalate the conflict at a mass meeting of teachers at City Hall with inflammatory rhetoric referring to the Ocean Hill board and McCoy as "black gangsters and Nazi types."[37] This demagoguery prompted the filmmaker Woody Allen to insert a remark about Shanker in his 1973 film *Sleeper*. When the hero awakens in a future world, he is informed that the old world was destroyed by a nuclear holocaust as a result of a man named Albert Shanker obtaining nuclear warheads.

Shanker was unrepentant about his inflammatory role. Two years later he commented on the subject of a massive reprinting of the anti-Semitic literature: "[You] don't mobilize the conscience of the city or the state of New York by making believe that this kind of garbage doesn't exist. . . . I think we're playing an educational role in trying to show people that this garbage exists."[38]

A generation later an apologist for the union would exonerate Shanker. Jim Sleeper would dismiss the fact that "Albert Shanker magnified such [anti-Semitic] rhetoric . . . because Jewish fear and resentment of blacks [was not] the racism of the old South."[39] Another journalist would take a more moderate view. In his 1988 analysis of the conflict, Jonathan Kaufman focused on "the collapse of the liberal coalition" that had existed between blacks and Jews.[40] He concluded that "today, the alliance lies in pieces."[41] Both accounts neglect to mention strains of racism in the Jewish community.

Some Jewish intellectuals criticized this strain of racism. Writing in the theological journal *Judaism* in the fall of 1969, young philosophy professor Michael Lerner would accuse the organized Jewish community of being "racist, internally corrupt, and an apologist for the worst aspects of American capitalism."[42] (Lerner would later, in the 1980s, become founder and editor of *Tikkun*, a respected Jewish liberal journal of opinion, and a confidante of President Bill Clinton.) Lerner focused his charges on "the phenomenon of 'black anti-Semitism'" upon which there seemed to him "an incredible concentration by almost every Jewish organization."[43] Although not dismissing the threat of black anti-Semitism, Lerner noted a cause that was "rooted in the concrete fact of oppression by Jews of blacks in the ghetto."[44] For Lerner, "the incredible relish" with which leaders of Jewish organizations reacted to "the slogan of" black anti-Semitism "legitimizes the racism" that had existed within certain members of the Jewish community.[45] He asked his readers to recall the "frequent references to 'the schwartzes' long before you ever heard about black anti-Semitism."[46] His attack brought forth a plethora of anguished rebuttals from readers and contributors to the journal.

A scholarly interpretation was offered by French political scientist Sophie Body-Gendrot. In her 1993 analysis of the conflict, she perceived the major responsibility to lie with UFT president Albert Shanker:

> The stroke of genius of Albert Shanker and his union was to shift the epicenter of the conflict by transforming a non-mobilizing controversy over "dismissal" and "transfer" of union teachers of Ocean Hill into a racial conflict. . . . Starting in September, the UFT ceased talking about the "job" issue and developed, using all means possible, everything that could arouse irrational fears, worries of racial origin in the New Yorkers, all towards agitating the specter of anti-Semitism among Jews. . . . The UFT made a rational negotiated solution impossible. . . .
>
> Shanker didn't hesitate to resort to the irregular blow even to get thrown in jail to win his battle. Falsifying facts, handing out to the press a picture of blacks brandishing knives, starting false rumors on television . . . knowingly disparaging the educational goals of Ocean Hill as imposed by Nazis, associating the community cause with the most virulent racist declaration by black activists mostly from outside the community. . . . [F]or Shanker, the risk of being unmasked weighed little compared to the gain of strategy. The support of the press is the best possible way to politicize the controversy and make it heard in a biased fashion.[47]

Body-Gendrot concluded that the "UFT's racist strategy" would result in "provoking a rapid polarization of race and class on the educational issue from which it has never lessened."[48]

In order to repair his image, Shanker made a brilliant move. He pressured the *New York Times* editorial staff to print as a paid advertisement a weekly column by him on education. It was the first time that the *Times*—or any major metropolitan newspaper—did so. Moreover, the column was to be published in the weekly "News in Review" section, the most analytical part of the paper. Chagrined by their early support of community control, the publishers of the *Times* felt obliged to depart from journalistic tradition. Shanker's column became the first major commentary on education by anyone in the United States in a major media outlet. Thoughtful and polemically tough, Shanker's columns enabled him to emerge as "a major, if not entirely welcome, force in American education," according to one observer.[49] With his ascendancy to the AFT presidency in 1974, Shanker was able to overcome his Ocean Hill reputation and, in the opinion of one educational observer, became "one of education's and the labor movement's most creative thinkers."[50] Later Shanker would align himself with the conservative educational reformers of the 1980s.

The battle over community control was decided by the state legislature. The union emerged as victor. Under union pressure, the New York State Legislature passed a decentralization bill that had little resemblance to community control. Most of the educational policymaking power remained with the central board. All citizens could vote in school elections. Most important, a complicated system of proportional representation was installed that favored slate voting and organized groups.

The first citywide school board elections in 1970 were disastrous. Slates proposed by the Catholic church dominated, with those proposed by the teachers' union coming in second. Consequently, the typical public school board member was a white, male, Catholic professional with two children in parochial schools.[51] By 1986, the UFT would dominate school board elections with twenty-five of thirty-two boards having majorities of union-backed candidates.[52] In a bitter irony, the UFT of the 1980s would resist the dismantling of decentralization advocated by some critics.

The UFT's success in controlling the legislative battle was due to two main factors. First, the union capitalized on its strong lobbying presence in the state capitol. Shanker promised to "follow every legislator around who voted [for the mayor's bill] and kill them politically."[53] The mayor's impact on the legislature was severely diminished with the emergence of black anti-Semitism, which attuned Shanker's racist strategy to fan the fears of many nonblack New Yorkers.

Second, Martin Mayer's polemical, one-sided account, *The Teachers Strike*, was published in full by *New York Times Magazine* in February and galvanized the legislature. Cited by lawmakers, the piece wielded great influence. Mayer exonerated the union and blamed McCoy and the "very ignorant" governing board and its allies at the Ford Foundation. This portrayal of the conflict was symptomatic of the New York press. A study by the Center for New York City Affairs revealed that members of the black community felt that the press failed "to report the community or governing board side of the dispute," ignoring "the positive aspect of [their] accomplishment" and portraying the school leaders as "racists and extreme black militants."[54]

MY INVOLVEMENT

I was to play a role in the community control movement. As an aide to Marilyn Gittell at the Institute for Community Studies at Queens College, I was extremely active in the struggle for community control. The institute was a conduit for funds for the operation of the experiments in community control, providing technical assistance.

The technical assistance provided by the institute covered a variety of services. First, educational aid was offered. As an example, teachers were exposed to the British Infant School method and traveled to Britain to observe that method firsthand. School administrators were provided expertise in administration through workshops conducted by nationally known consultants. Second, the institute provided public relations assistance so that the besieged school boards could convey their message to the public. And, finally, the institute helped manage the added funds allocated to the community school boards by the Ford Foundation.

Although I was from an academic family (my uncle and legal guardian was a professor at Fordham University), I spent seventeen years (from 1957 to 1973) primarily as a social activist. Scholarship was to come later. First, I was a member of a radical Catholic labor group, the Association of Catholic Trade Unionists, which fought labor racketeering and aided poor Puerto Ricans in New York. I was the editor of the organization's publication, the *Labor Leader*, and also functioned as an organizer. During the latter assignment, I was jailed briefly during a boycott of a racketeer union.

Later I joined the Socialist Party and wrote for its official organ *New America* and the socialist journal *New Politics*. During that time, I was assistant editor of the UFT's newspaper, during Albert Shanker's tenure, and was part of a select group of labor intellectuals, formed by Michael Harrington, to have monthly discussions on social issues (one such was a debate on Black Power between Bayard Rustin and Floyd McKissick). I resigned from the Socialist Party in 1968 over the issue of community control. The active stance against community control taken by Harrington and such Rustin aides as Tom Kahn and Sandra Feldman (who was later to become UFT president) precipitated my decision. My resignation letter to Harrington, then national chairman of the Socialist Party, read as follows:

For one who is actively engaged in stimulating equality of educational opportunity to do battle with fellow comrades, who are as actively promoting the temporary (I hope) racist policies of the UFT in its fight against school decentralization and to remain in a party that unofficially is opposed to school decentralization would be unconscionable.[55]

The previous year I had left the union over community control. When I had covered the I.S. 201 boycott in the union newspaper, I had written in a piece entitled "Black Power Comes to Schools" that "This is what black power intends: a measure of self government, of participatory democracy.... For these youngsters ... black power is more than a slogan."[56]

After a year as an educational aide in Mayor Lindsay's newly created Office of Educational Liaison, which served to promote decentralization, I joined Gittell at the Institute for Community Studies where I directed its publication arm, publishing a newsletter, articles, and monographs on community control. I also served as a researcher contributing to three published studies on community control. In addition to providing technical assistance to the experiments, I wrote over a dozen articles and book reviews on the subject for such intellectual journals as the Catholic lay journal *Commonweal* and *New Politics*.

Perhaps my key contribution was an edited reader on the Ocean Hill conflict, *Confrontation at Ocean Hill–Brownsville*, published in May of 1969. The book has become a standard reference work on the issue. My intent was to present both sides of the debate that had been published in intellectual journals. I asked Marilyn Gittell to be co-editor. Although offering both sides of the issue, we wrote an introductory essay arguing for community control. We selected countering pieces even though the liberal and radical observers had overwhelmingly supported the community control movement by a ratio of three to one. Gittell's contribution was significant both conceptually and editorially. She suggested that we also published the documents to the conflict such as the report of the American Civil Liberties Union supporting Ocean Hill and the anti-Semitic literature. We had hoped to influence the legislature, but Martin Mayer's piece in *New York Times Magazine* was published prior to our book. When Gittell disbanded the institute in 1973, I became less active in social issues and turned to scholarship.

MARILYN GITTELL

Marilyn Gittell played a large role in the community control struggle. She had established her scholarly and liberal credentials. As a policy advisor to the Bundy panel, she wielded considerable influence in that study. And as the director of the Institute for Community Studies, which she founded in 1967, she provided assistance and advice to the experimental districts.

Her efforts won her national recognition as a major educational reformer. In their 1973 book on school reform, *The School Book*, educators Neil Postman and Charles Weingartner characterized Gittell as an advocate for the underdog. They described her as "largely associated with the fight for community control of schools" and "through her books . . . her solid research, and her active participation in political battles, she has established herself as an implacable enemy of bureaucracy, and like Boston Blackie, a friend to those who have no friends."[57]

Gittell's political philosophy and subsequent activism can best be described as that of a liberal who, when confronted by the evidence, arrived at radical conclusions. In her first study, she assumed as her working hypothesis the mainstream analyses of such social scientists as Robert Dahl and Edward Banfield that American politics was dominated by a consensus arrived at by a plethora of influential interest groups. However, when she studied the New York City school system she found the opposite: an unaccountable bureaucracy dominated by professionals with little input from interest groups. Her conclusion that urban school systems suffered from a pathology of bureaucracy was in line with the writings of sociologist Max Weber. Never affiliated with any radical political group, she remained an independent thinker whose counsel to the experimental board was reasoned and did not at all urge them to extremist actions as intimated by critics such as Michael Harrington and Martin Mayer.

A young professor of political science at the outbreak of the Ocean Hill confrontation, Gittell was 38. Married to a professional with two accounting firms, and the mother of two children, she founded the Institute for Community Studies primarily as an activist think tank on community control. She received a Ford Foundation grant of $1 million to provide assistance to the experimental school boards. Part of that grant also authorized scholarly studies of these boards. She published two such studies: *Local Control in Education* and *School Boards and School Policy*, of which I was a co-author. She designed the studies, employed researchers on her staff to gather data, and interpreted the results. Gittell was one of the first to use qualititative methods as well as quantitative methods. She employed participant observers on the school boards. In this respect, she was quite ahead of her time in social science research. Gittell would eventually publish fourteen books on participation and education, and she received city and federal grants in the millions.

With the demise of community control, Gittell disbanded the institute and went on to become an academic vice-president at her alma mater, Brooklyn College. But she was not to move into higher education without some controversy. Again, New York was to witness another demagogic outburst by UFT president Albert Shanker. In his paid *New York Times* column, Shanker lambasted City University chancellor Robert Kibbee for having

mounted a new offensive directed at teachers, parents and community boards of the city's public school system . . . by promoting Dr. Marilyn Gittell to the post of Associate Provost . . . [a decision] not of merit and excellence but that of outstanding proficiency in the field of extremist politics. Marilyn Gittell was a major architect of the 1968 Ocean Hill–Brownsville controversy. . . . Kibbee's promotion of Gittell is as well-advised as, let us say, the appointment of a white supremacist as director of the university's Black Studies program.[58]

Moreover, Shanker made an appearance at the Board of Higher Education's meeting on the appointment. Reverting to his favorite tactic of equating Gittell, whose civil rights role was unquestioned, to white racists, Shanker called the board action "the equivalent of the appointment of George Wallace as head of the Brooklyn College Education Department."[59] In addition, he notified the board that the appointment would do no less than "threaten the entire relation that exists between our union and the City University."[60]

Shanker clearly embarrassed the *New York Times*. Consequently, the editors sought damage control. They published an editorial that, on the one hand, chastised Shanker for having "injected a longstanding ideological feud with Dr. Gittell . . . that is entirely outside his jurisdiction" and, on the other hand, tarnished Gittell's scholarship by portraying her as "having always rejected the posture of the uninvolved scholar."[61]

With poetic justice five years later, *Change* magazine, a respected journal of higher education, would list Gittell as one of their "100 Young Leaders of the Academy."[62] Parenthetically, two others mentioned, William Bennett and Chester E. Finn, Jr., at the ideologically opposite pole from Gittell, would make their presence felt in American education a decade later.

HISTORICAL ASSESSMENT

The historical image of the community control movement is that, according to Diane Ravitch, it "failed politically."[63] However, the experiments proved to be educationally successful. Gittell's study of the experimental boards, *Local Control in Education*, documented that success.

First, the experimental boards were reflective of the black and Hispanic school population. The typical board member was a black female with high school education, a poverty worker or paraprofessional with children in the public schools. The school board elections had a 25 percent participation rate that compared favorably with suburban boards. For the first time in a major city, superintendents and principals were black, Hispanic, and Chinese. Community school boards devoted a greater portion of their time to educational policy than suburban boards did. Dissatisfied with academic performance, they sought improvements. Moreover, poor parents attended on average three to five PTA meetings a year, a higher rate than before in New York City.

Educationally, the boards launched innumerable innovative programs such as the first bilingual program in the North. Students experienced heightened feelings of fate control and performed at higher academic levels than students affiliated with similar boards in other economically deprived areas. Finally, the members of these boards developed educational and political expertise.[64]

Currently, reflective and responsible historians have equally perceived the importance of the community control struggle. From France, Body-Gendrot, in her study *Ville et Violence*, assessed the episode as one that energized the black community politically. In a similar vein, American historian of the Black Power movement William L. Van De Burg, in his study *New Day in Babylon,* presented a favorable portrait of community control. He characterized the community control activists as attempting to participate in "existing institutions and creating new ones to meet their special needs" so that "black parents would counteract the social-ization in whiteness" endemic to traditional schooling.[65] In doing so these activists, said Van De Burg, would assure "that the concept—and perhaps the reality—of Black Power was passed on to the next genera-tion."[66]

De Burg dismissed those critics who argued that community control would result in resegregation, political factional fighting over limited spoils, and a "reversion to tribalism." Instead, he concluded that

Black Power energized and educated black Americans, introducing many to the concept of political pluralism. It spurred new interest in African liberation strug-gles and the plight of the powerless worldwide. Newly sensitized to the political nature of oppression, Black Power converts set out to remedy the situation by forming numerous political-action caucuses and grass roots community associ-ations. These, in turn, served as often-utilized models for the various ethnic, gender, and class consciousness movements of the seventies and eighties.[67]

How have African Americans viewed the community control struggle? Perhaps the best guide has been the award-winning television documen-tary *Eyes on the Prize,* produced by Henry Hampton. Using *cinema verité* techniques of current interviews interspersed with actual historical foot-age, *Eyes on the Prize* documents the civil rights struggle in both the South and the North spanning the period from the 1950s to 1990. The northern segment had as its third episode a segment entitled "Power (1966–1968)." This episode contained three stories: the election of the first Af-rican-American mayor of a major city (Cleveland), Carl Stokes; the rise of the Black Panther Party; and a twenty-two minute segment on Ocean Hill–Brownsville. The video presented both sides of the conflict at Ocean Hill. Nevertheless the documentary firmly argued that the community control experiment in Ocean Hill was a "means to improve the quality of the education of their children, to boost the self-image of Black and Hispanic students, to bring more minority teachers into the schools, and to make the curriculum more relevant to minority students."[68]

History is often cruel. Consequently, it is understandable that some liberals and radicals opposed to the community control movement would modify their views as time passed. Criticized for their support of the teachers' union, these opponents of community control significantly altered their earlier views. The most influential of these was the socialist Michael Harrington. Harrington had established himself with his po-lemic on poverty, *The Other America,* published in 1962, which "rediscovered" massive poverty and launched a federal program. Moreover, Harrington had close ties to Rev. Martin Luther King, Jr.

In the community control struggle, he was not only an advisor to Shanker but wrote the most devastating critique of community control, one whose arguments were to be repeated by liberals, radicals, and conservatives alike. For Harrington, the blame rested mostly with those white supporters, especially the foundation staff and Mayor Lindsay, who "eminently qualified . . . as members . . . of corporate liberalism" to unite against the poor and working class.[69] In short, Harrington employed a tortured logic to make the white middle-class teachers the victims. He wrote that community control was a "reactionary shell game" imposed "at the expense of the poor in Ocean Hill–Brownsville" so that "these very same corporate chiefs are right now planning an increase in unemployment in order to protect the stability of prices and the worth of the dollar."[70]

This paranoiac flight from reasoning was echoed by others. Socialist scholar Stanley Aronowitz declared that "the foundations serve the interests of corporate capital and they promote community involvement in order to . . . [train] the labor force to meet the requirements of the production system."[71]

Both Harrington and Aronowitz preferred a Civil Rights Movement that was less assertive. Harrington had long argued that political participation was not a viable solution for the poor since the research indicated the poor were too alienated to participate.

Twenty years later he would modify his views. In the second installment of his autobiography, Harrington reflected: "I supported the union, yet I was all but torn in two by my profound sympathies with those on the other side who, I thought, were morally right, legally wrong, and very ill advised by theorists from outside their community."[72] Interestingly, Harrington chose the "legal" over the "moral" right, condemning "outsiders" in the same fashion that white racist southerners would condemn northern liberal outsiders.

Responding to Harrington's charges, Marilyn Gittell declared that the community school boards decided their own fate:

As far as I know, the local people on those community boards made their own decisions. Mario Fantini [of the Ford Foundation] and I occasionally disagreed with some of the decisions made by Rhody McCoy and the Ocean Hill board. But it was essentially their show. Michael Harrington and the other critics of our role were merely trying to rationalize their non-support of the black community by blaming me, Mario and the Ford Foundation.[73]

Aronowitz would also soften his views. On the twentieth anniversary of the Ocean Hill confrontation, Aronowitz declared that for school reform "the real action remains in the neighborhoods [as it was among the black parents in Ocean Hill–Brownsville in 1968] where some parents have gotten up the courage to buck the conservative tide."[74] For these socialists, siding against African Americans was especially difficult.

Diane Ravitch also made a significant revisionist interpretation. In her 1974 book *The Great School Wars*, prompted by the Ocean Hill controversy, she concluded that "the drive for community control was a direct assault on the idea of the common school."[75] For Ravitch, "the common school idea . . . has survived because it is appropriate to a democratic, heterogeneous society."[76] A decade later, she would find positive value in the community control movement: "Ironically, . . . the community control movement left as its legacy the conviction that blacks must not be seen as an inferior caste, to be pitied and despised, but an ethnic group asserting its demands and interests like others in a pluralistic society."[77]

For Gittell, the major lesson of the community control movement was political. In 1993, she reflected that "The Ocean Hill confrontation points out the need for democracy to be constantly vigilant so as to be more inclusive and more participating. We can't allow professionals alone to make decisions affecting people's lives."[78]

CONCLUSION

What was the legacy of the community control movement? First, it had enormous racial implications. As one of the earliest expressions of Black Power, community control gave African Americans a new image. Blacks would determine their own fate, direct their own Civil Rights Movement, and rediscover their own useable past. Most important, it signified the end of African Americans regarding themselves as inferior players in the politics of American education.

Second, community control had lasting educational significance. For the first time, parental involvement—much discussed by educators—became a policy issue. It was to have long-range influence on American education. Milbrey Wallin McLaughlin and Patrick M. Shields, in their review of twenty years of parental involvement, reported that the evidence on "advisory" programs of involvement was "mixed" and dependent on implementation. They concluded that "most strategies for parental involvement have not been carried out as intended."[79] By the 1980s, site-based management became extremely popular in school reform. In site-based management, decision making is determined on a school level by a committee comprised of the principal, teachers, and parents.

Finally, community control had an impact on the American political fabric, for it raised the ultimate question of a democratic society: Can everyone participate in the political process, or is participation to be restricted to merely an affluent, educated few? Never again were the poor to be so dramatically and energetically championed. Community control is rightly judged as an important chapter in the history of the Civil Rights Movement in the United States.

NOTES

1. Kwame Ture (Stokely Carmichael) and Charles V. Hamilton, *Black Power: The Politics of Liberation* (New York; Vintage Edition, 1992), p. 187.

2. Daniel P. Moynihan, *Maximum Feasible Misunderstanding* (New York: Free Press, 1969), p. xvi.

3. Alan Adelson, *SDS* (New York: Charles Scribner's Sons, 1972), p. 2.

4. *Ibid.*

5. Ture and Hamilton, *Black Power*, p. 47.

6. *Ibid.*

7. Preston R. Wilcox, "The Controversy Over I.S. 201," *The Urban Review* (Center for Urban Education), July 1966, p. 13.

8. *Ibid.*

9. Ture and Hamilton, *Black Power*, pp. 166, 171.

10. Frederick O. Hayes, memorandum to Richard Boone et al., New York City Office of the Mayor, January 21, 1969, p. 2.

11. Maurice R. Berube and Marilyn Gittell, eds., *Confrontation at Ocean Hill–Brownsville* (New York: Praeger, 1969), pp. 3–4.

12. *Ibid.*, p. 3.

13. Martin Mayer, *The Teachers Strike* (New York: Harper & Row, 1968), pp. 27, 112.

14. *Ibid.*, p. 114.

15. Naomi Levine with Richard Cohen, *Ocean Hill–Brownsville: A Case History of Schools in Crisis* (New York: Popular Library, 1969), p. 153.

16. *Ibid.*

17. Hayes, memorandum, p. 4.

18. Moynihan, *Maximum Feasible Misunderstanding*, p. 191.

19. *Ibid.*

20. Maurice R. Berube, "Black Power Comes to School," *The United Teacher*, September 22, 1966, p. 6.

21. Henry Hampton and Steve Fayer, *Voices of Freedom: An Oral History of the Civil Rights Movement from the 1950's through the 1980's* (New York: Bantam Books, 1990), p. 502.

22. Kimberly R. Vann and Jawanza Kunjufu, "The Importance of an Afrocentric, Multicultural Curriculum," *Phi Delta Kappan*, February 1993, p. 490.

23. *Ibid.*

24. Wilcox, "The Controversy," p. 13.

25. *Ibid.*

26. Berube and Gittell, eds., *Confrontation at Ocean Hill–Brownsville*, p. 82.

27. Ture and Hamilton, *Black Power*, p. 171.

28. Jonathan Kaufman, *Broken Alliance: The Turbulent Times Between Blacks and Jews in America* (New York: Charles Scribner's Sons, 1988), p. 133.

29. Manning Marable, *Race, Reform and Rebellion: The Second Reconstruction in Black America, 1945–1990* (Jackson: University Press of Mississippi, 1991), p. 118.

30. Melvin Urofsky, ed., *Why Teachers Strike: Teacher Rights and Community Control* (New York: Anchor Books, 1970), p. 177.

31. *Newsweek*, April 19, 1993, p. 49.

32. Sophie Body-Gendrot, *Ville et Violence* (Paris: Presses Universitaires de France, 1993), p. 104, translation by the author.

33. "The Burden of the Blame: NYCIU Report on the Ocean Hill–Brownsville School Controversy," in Berube and Gittell, eds., *Confrontation at Ocean Hill–Brownsville*, p. 104.

34. Mayer, *The Teachers Strike*, p. 15.

35. *New York Times*, October 30, 1968, p. 33.

36. David Selden, *The Teacher Rebellion* (Washington, D.C.: Howard University Press, 1985), p. 153.

37. Berube and Gittell, eds., *Confrontation at Ocean Hill–Brownsville*, p. 146.

38. Urofsky, ed., *Why Teachers Strike*, p. 160.

39. Jim Sleeper, *The Closest of Strangers: Liberalism and the Politics of Race in New York* (New York: W. W. Norton, 1990), pp. 21, 100.

40. Kaufman, *Broken Alliance*, p. 7.

41. *Ibid.*

42. Michael Lerner, "Jewish New Leftism at Berkeley," *Judaism*, Fall 1969, p. 475.

43. *Ibid.*

44. *Ibid.*

45. *Ibid.*, p. 476.

46. *Ibid.*

47. Body-Gendrot, *Ville et Violence*, pp. 102–103, translation by Bouziane Mohsin and the author.

48. *Ibid.*, p. 107.

49. George R. Kaplan, "Shining Lights in High Places: Education's Top Four Leaders and Their Heirs," *Phi Delta Kappan*, September 1985, p. 12.

50. *Ibid.*, p. 13.

51. Marilyn Gittell with Maurice R. Berube et al., *School Boards and School Policy: An Evaluation of Decentralization in New York City* (New York: Praeger, 1973), p. 91.

52. Maurice R. Berube, *Teacher Politics: The Influence of Unions* (Westport, Conn.: Greenwood Press, 1988), p. 73.

53. Sol Stern, " 'Scab' Teachers," in Berube and Gittell, eds., *Confrontation at Ocean Hill–Brownsville*, p. 185.

54. George Barner, *The Ocean Hill–Brownsville Community Views the News Coverage* (New York: Center for New York City Affairs, December 1968).

55. Maurice R. Berube, letter to Michael Harrington, chairman, Socialist Party, September 13, 1968.

56. Berube, "Black Power Comes to Schools," p. 6.

57. Neil Postman and Charles Weingartner, *The School Book* (New York: Delacorte Press, 1973), p. 218.

58. Albert Shanker, "Can Kibbee Lead the Fight for Free Tuition?" *New York Times*, December 2, 1973, p. E11.

59. *New York Times*, January 13, 1974, p. 64.

60. *Ibid.*

61. *New York Times*, January 15, 1974, p. 36.

62. "100 Young Leaders of the Academy," *Change*, October 1978, p. 29.

63. Diane Ravitch, *The Troubled Crusade: American Education 1945–1980* (New York: Basic Books, 1983), p. 174.

64. Marilyn Gittell with Maurice R. Berube et al., *Local Control in Education: Three Demonstration School Districts in New York City* (New York: Praeger, 1972).

65. William L. Van De Burg, *New Day in Babylon: The Black Power Movement in America* (Chicago: University of Chicago Press, 1992), p. 124.

66. *Ibid.*

67. *Ibid.*, p. 306.

68. Hampton and Fayer, *Voices of Freedom*, p. 486.

69. Michael Harrington, "An Open Letter to Men of Good Will (with an aside to Dwight MacDonald)," in Berube and Gittell, eds., *Confrontation at Ocean Hill–Brownsville*, p. 236.

70. *Ibid.*

71. Stanley Aronowitz, "A Reply to Maurice R. Berube's 'Social Change and the White Working Class,'" *Social Policy*, September/October 1970, p. 40.

72. Michael Harrington, *The Long Distance Runner: An Autobiography* (New York: Holt, 1988), p. 77.

73. Interview with Marilyn Gittell, director, Howard Samuels Policy Institute, City University of New York, New York City, November 19, 1993 (telephone).

74. Stanley Aronowitz and Henry A. Giroux, "Hope for Our Schools: A New Manifesto for Education," *Village Voice*, October 4, 1988, p. 121.

75. Diane Ravitch, *The Great School Wars* (New York: Basic Books, 1974), p. 397.

76. *Ibid.*, p. 402.

77. Ravitch, *The Troubled Crusade*, p. 174.

78. Interview with Marilyn Gittell.

79. Milbrey Wallin McLaughlin and Patrick M. Shields, "Involving Low-Income Parents in the Schools: A Role for Policy," *Phi Delta Kappan*, October 1987, p. 157.

CHAPTER SIX

THE DRIFT TO PRIVATIZATION

The third great school reform movement began in the early 1980s and was dubbed the excellence reform movement. It was triggered by the U.S. Department of Education's 1983 report *A Nation at Risk: The Imperative for Educational Reform*, written by the National Commission on Excellence in Education. The essence of excellence reform was raising the standards and performance of public school children in the United States. Excellence reform focused on helping the best and brightest to compete in the global market. The assumption of the excellence reformers was that U.S. public schools had failed, and only comprehensive systemic reform was the answer. However, their condemnation of public schooling led many to advocate the alternative of private education and, ultimately, the privatization of American public education by corporations.

The matrix of excellence reform was economic. Never was there so clear a link between reform and an outside societal force. The decline of the U.S. economy, one of the world's most dominant, since the 1970s has been well documented. The United States dropped from second to fifth place in per capita gross national product (GNP), its industrial growth had slowed to 1 percent annually, and its trade deficit made it the largest debtor nation in the world.[1] Moreover, U.S. industrial investment declined from 3.3 percent to 2.3 percent,[2] and the federal government hampered economic recovery with its trillion-dollar national debt.

Reasons for this economic decline were complex. For one thing, American business made bad decisions, such as building large automobiles for a fuel-conscious worldwide public. Also, global competition meant that labor costs were cheaper in newly developed countries. Moreover, some charged that the U.S. labor force lacked the work ethic of the Great Depression generation that preceded it. Others noted that America's best scientists were in the space and defense industries.[3] America's global military presence was questioned as contributing to the federal budget deficit as our competitors, notably Japan and West Germany, maintained minimal armed forces. Most crucial, however, was the rise of global economic competition.

A Nation at Risk touched a raw nerve in the body politic, which was anxious about the nation's economic health. For the public it seemed easier to focus on educational reform than business reform. A consensus emerged whereby media, educational groups, business, and the public sought to restore America's allegedly failing schools and, in turn, improve the nation's economic well-being. *A Nation at Risk* begins by declaring that "our nation is at risk" because "our once unchallenged preeminence in commerce, industry, science, and technological innovation is being overtaken by competitors throughout the world."[4] It goes on to clearly connect the need for education reform with the failing U.S. economy:

History is not kind to idlers. The time is long past when America's destiny was assured simply by an abundance of natural resources and inexhaustible human enthusiasm, and by our relative isolation from the malignant problems of older civilizations. The world is indeed one global village. We live among determined, well-educated, and strongly motivated competitors. We compete with them for international standing and markets, not only with products but also with the ideas of our laboratories and neighborhood workshops. America's position in the world may once have been reasonably secure with only a few exceptionally well-trained men and women. It is no longer.

The risk is not only that the Japanese make automobiles more efficiently than Americans and have government subsidies for development and export. It is not just that the South Koreans recently built the world's most efficient steel mill, or that American machine tools, once the pride of the world, are being displaced by German products. It is also that these developments signify a redistribution of trained capability throughout the globe. Knowledge, learning, information, and skilled intelligence are the new raw materials of international commerce and are today spreading throughout the world as vigorously as miracle drugs, synthetic fertilizers, and blue jeans did earlier. . . .

Learning is the indispensable investment required for success in the "information age" we are entering.[5]

Other reports confirmed *A Nation at Risk*'s contention that "education is correlated with economic and social development."[6] For example, a report on education by business and university leaders presented to President Reagan at the same time of *A Nation at Risk* had but one recommendation, namely, that "as a nation we must develop a consensus that industrial competition is crucial to our social and economic well-being."[7]

Some educators demurred from that view. Clark Kerr, former chancellor of the California higher education system, disputed the link between better education and economic growth. Citing studies by the Massachusetts Institute of Technology, Princeton University, and the Brookings Institution, Kerr noted a weak correlation between productivity and improved education.[8] And Larry Cuban, former president of the American Educational Research Association, challenged the assumption that school reform would translate into rescuing a faltering economy. "Schools are important," he argued, "but not critical to economic competitiveness in a global economy."[9] Cuban cited other factors for America's economic decline: "other countries' use of low-wage, less-educated workers and new technologies to make competitively priced products; from American firms' increasing tendency to global, in production and marketing; from the growth of the services sector over the manufacturing sector; and from just plain errors in judgment."[10]

For the most part, these views were the exception rather than the rule. The large majority of the educational establishment as well as the political and business community believed otherwise. And they were joined by most of the American public.

BUSINESS AS AN EDUCATION POLICY MAKER

With the ushering in of excellence reform, the romance between business and education was underway. Most educators were glad that "business has rediscovered the schools" and that "of all the recent changes in the landscape of American education, none has been more dramatic and swift than the reappearance of the business sector."[11] Michael Timpane, president of Teachers College, Columbia University, went further by cautioning that it was "education's best alternative ... to accept and work with business *zestfully*" (emphasis added).[12]

For its part, the corporate sector took up school reform with messianic fervor. Concerned about America's economic decline, business leaders were convinced that school reform was a means to restore U.S. technological superiority and provide a capable workforce. The business press reflected this perception that corporate America would become education's saving remnant with a steady drumbeat of articles. *Business Week* declared the mission of U.S. corporations as no less than "Saving Our Schools"; *Forbes* proclaimed that "When Our Schools Do Badly, So Does America"; *Nation's Business* would define "Business Initiatives for Better Schools"; and *Fortune* in one of its annual education summits since 1987 focused on "How to Help America's Schools."

What this ferment signified was a change in educational policy making. One analyst cheered that "the major players in American business mean to become movers and shakers in school policy."[13] Whereas U.S. business was largely absent from the equity reform movement with its social goals, it now felt pressed to involve itself in a reform movement molded by economic considerations.

The business community became involved in school policy and education reform in myriad ways. First, corporate panels by 1990 issued some 300 reports on American education. National government policy panels as well as state governmental forums were well represented by corporate leaders. The former chairman of Xerox, David Kearns, became a top educational aide in the Bush administration. And President Bush's school reform strategy, America 2000, carved out a role of business. Bush's plan called for alternate certification for school administrators that would permit business executives to manage schools. For example, in the fall of 1993, the Minneapolis school board hired a management consultant with no prior educational experience to be superintendent.[14] The governor of California did the same for the state's superintendent position.[15]

Corporate America responded by creating an umbrella organization, Business Coalition for Education, that represented eleven business groups. These included the Business Roundtable, the U.S. Chamber of Commerce, the National Alliance for Business, the National Association of Manufacturers, and the Committee for Economic Development, among others. Finally, chief executive officers (CEOs) of major corporations testified regularly on federal education legislation.[16] A number of businesses hired education specialists to conduct studies of public schooling. One educational analyst perceived the role of business as a social engineer in school reform to be inevitable, the only question being "whether the new look is more like a hostile takeover or a productive merger."[17]

And business did take a lead in school reform. A survey in 1991 by *Fortune* magazine of the CEOs of the 500 largest industrial firms and the 500 largest service corporations indicated the interest business had in education. Of the 301 corporate executives who responded, 41 percent claimed that they were "very involved" in educational reform, and 42 percent responded that they were "fairly involved."[18] However, in interpreting the survey, *Fortune* noted that "in some cases it's the employees, not their bosses, who best illustrate a company's involvement."[19] However, the CEOs were disappointed with the impact of their involvement. Only 10 percent perceived that business support resulted in a "big difference" in how schools operated, and 46 percent considered that business made a "fair amount of difference."[20] A total of 144 corporations reported providing financial assistance to education, much of it to higher education. These corporations were among U.S. giants, including, among others, AT&T, Bank America, Chrysler, Coca Cola, Dow Chemical, IBM, Exxon, General Electric, General Motors, Xerox, Union Carbide, Polaroid, Eastman Kodak, Ford and Merrill Lynch.

THE NIXON PRECEDENT

President George Bush made a point of including business in the national education reform movement. In his America 2000 strategy for education reform, he directed "American business leaders [to] establish— and muster the private resources for—the New American Schools Development Corporation [NASDC]."[21] NASDC would raise $150 million to $200 million "to jump start the R&D teams" that would design 535 New American Schools of an innovative nature that would serve as national models breaking the mold of existent public schooling.[22] NASDC would award contracts to 7 research and development "think tanks, school innovators, management consultants, and others."[23] The research and development teams, in turn, would have the "mission . . . to help communities to create schools that will reach the national education goals."[24]

Bush's "break the mold" schools echoed an earlier policy thrust of President Richard Nixon, the Experimental Schools Program. The Nixon program provided local school districts with $55 million for a six-year period from 1970 to 1976 to seek "comprehensive change." The program failed and, according to one critic, "passed into history without substantially improving existing knowledge."[25] Scholars are divided as to the reasons for the failure. Michael Kirst argued that these schools "flopped" because "there was no adequate research base for the programs."[26] Similarly, he questioned the New American Schools project as being "long on development and short on a research strategy to find comparative effectiveness."[27] Diane Ravitch considered the Nixon initiative "one of the most ambitious federal efforts to reform the schools."[28] However, she once again criticized the goal of "comprehensive change." For Ravitch, "neither federal nor local officials knew what comprehensive change meant."[29] Ravitch wondered "how, then, did piecemeal change get such a bad reputation."[30] Moreover, she deplored the Nixon administration's "insistence on community involvement" as multiplying "the number of interests" that "further frustrated the possibility of coherent, comprehensive educational change."[31] It is with some irony that Ravitch, who held comprehensive change suspect in the equity reform movement, would champion it in the excellence reform movement as Assistant Secretary of Research in the Bush Department of Education.

BUSINESS PARTNERSHIPS

Corporate America has provided monetary support to education in a number of ways. Partnerships with the schools have been increasingly common whereby business gives financial support to specific schools and school districts. In a four-year period alone, between 1984 and 1988, these partnerships rose dramatically from 42,300 to 124,800.[32] However, the business arrangement with the potential for corporate America to have the most direct influence has been the compact.

The first compact was arranged in Boston in 1982. Local businesses in conjunction with universities entered into a contractual five-year agreement with the Boston public school system. Under the terms of the agreement, some 400 Boston businesses would guarantee high school graduates summer and entry-level jobs, while universities would provide scholarships. In return, the public schools were expected to improve school performance, namely, to reduce absenteeism, and dropout rates, to increase student academic scores and to enlarge the pool of students able to enter college.

Known as the Boston Compact, the partnership became a model for the rest of the nation. It had mixed results. Businesses and the college community made good on their pledges. Some 3,000 students were given summer jobs and 1,000 students permanent jobs.[33] Universities offered $2.5 million in scholarships.[34] Indeed, in 1986 the unemployment rate for Boston high school graduates was only 5 percent compared to a national average of 19.6 percent.[35] On the other hand, the Boston school system failed to deliver its end of the bargain. School performance did not rise significantly, and corporate leaders saw the need for more accountability.

The experiment of the Boston Compact raised the issue of corporate control of education. Educational observer Marilee C. Rist considered the Boston Compact the "symbol of a significant change" whereby business was transformed from "donor, sponsor, and supporter to reform engineer."[36] She posed the ultimate question: "What is a proper role for business in improving schools? Is it appropriate for business to decide what curriculum works best? And is it right that business—by virtue of its political and financial power—imposes its solutions on schools?"[37] For Rist, the answer was a resounding yes.

The Boston Compact spurred on the National Alliance for Business (NAB) to other compact experiments. In 1986, the NAB initiated compacts in twelve cities in two stages. In the first round of compacts, seven cities were involved: Albuquerque, Cincinnati, Indianapolis, Louisville, Memphis, San Diego, and Seattle. In the next year five more cities were added: Detroit, Miami/Dade County, Pittsburgh, Providence, and Rochester. The goal of the NAB compacts was "academic improvements on the part of schools and at-risk students" for which "employers were asked to pledge job opportunities."[38]

A final report in 1991 reported limited success. Only two cities—Louisville and Cincinnati—registered school improvement as measured by the reduced dropout rate, increased school attendance, and higher scores on standardized tests. In San Diego, "the lack of business involvement" forced the school district to seek necessary funding from foundations and government.[39] Nevertheless, the NAB claimed success in the more nebulous areas of "improved communication and understanding."[40] Consequently, the NAB recommended that future compacts focus on the "whole student" with a "comprehensive program" that would address "the multiple factors in a student's life that have put that student at risk."[41]

One problem with the compacts has been their lack of structure and clear direction. Donald M. Clark criticized this "lack of substance" in business/school partnerships as a result of "unstructured, narrowly focused efforts."[42] Again, he sounded the call for a "comprehensive program of school reform" that would require "business leaders to play a more direct (and broader) role in local schools."[43] He suggested local industry-education councils.

Another area of business involvement has been providing the schools with technological hardware. Perhaps the most notable of these arrangements has been the IBM Writing to Read program. This program provides expensive computer laboratories to aid kindergarten, first-, and second-grade students in reading and writing. The computer laboratories range in cost from $24,000 to $65,000 per school given the size of the class.[44] The allure of computers has been popular with school superintendents anxious to show the latest technology in their systems. Computers have been used also with poor and minority students. However, research indicates that the Writing to Read programs have had negligible results.

Reviewing twenty-nine of these studies, Robert E. Slavin found "no positive effects" and "no difference in reading performances" in kindergarten, first-grade, and second-grade Writing to Read students than those in traditional classrooms.[45] There were some positive benefits on writing ability. However, Slavin explained these by the fact that traditionally kindergartners and first graders were not taught writing. He concluded that "given its modest . . . impact on reading, and its expense . . . one must wonder why Writing to Read has been so widely adopted."[46] Slavin suspected a "darker reason."[47] He ascribed the belief to some school boards, that "if only IBM or some other successful corporation could be put in charge of the schools, it would turn them around."[48]

One such evaluation (which I directed as a doctoral dissertation) not only confirmed Slavin's interpretation but illustrated the politics of reform. Ann-Carol Banton Holley evaluated two urban kindergarten programs in Norfolk, Virginia. This was shortly after Norfolk abandoned school busing for integration. One of the schools Holley studied employed the IBM Writing to Read program and the other a whole language approach that did not use computers and consisted mainly of retraining teachers in that method. Both schools served poor, minority student populations. Holley's sample was comprised of 128 kindergartners who were tested orally for their reading ability and their attitudes toward reading. She concluded that "the sixty-one whole language and sixty-seven Writing to Read students did not differ significant in their oral reading performance."[49] Moreover, she observed that, regardless of family background, "the whole language students had statistically significant better attitudes toward learning."[50]

The evaluation was presented to the superintendent of schools, Dr. Gene Carter, an African American who had recently been selected by the Association of American School Superintendents as an outstanding national educational leader. I also discussed the study with Carter. Carter had been chosen as the Norfolk superintendent when that city was dismantling integrated schools. He had approved the school boards' action despite criticism from the city's civil rights leaders. Carter largely ignored Holley's evaluation and expanded the Writing to Read program in the resegregated, all black "community schools" in Norfolk.[51]

In an effort to control the influence of business in education, the Association for Supervision and Curriculum Development issued in 1989 a set of "guidelines for business involvement in the schools."[52] ASCD leaders adopted a skeptical position, holding that "sometimes the interests of business coincide with those of public education, and sometimes they do not."[53] ASCD warned that often corporate America established school relations mainly for improving public relations of business rather than being sincerely interested in trying to improve student performance.[54] Most important, ASCD worried about business's influence on curriculum. The organization noted that materials provided by business, on a number of topics ranging from economic to environmental issues, have reflected bias and "have been especially controversial in the past."[55] Consequently, ASCD cautioned school boards that business's role in their school systems should be "structured": "Given that potential to influence educational change, either positively or negatively, it is important that educators attempt to structure business involvement in educational policymaking in ways that best promote student welfare."[56] One reads "structured" as a synonym for control. ASCD reflected the fears that, in the rush to invite business into their school systems, school board members might relinquish authority. Therefore, ASCD developed a set of guiding principles. Educators should ensure that the proposed involvement:

• is consistent with the values, goals and objectives of the educational program;
• responds to a clearly understood educational need;
• supports and does not undermine either implicitly or explicitly an existing curriculum and instruction message;
• has been considered and assessed by groups with different views.

In addition, the process should provide for an ongoing review of all school-business relationships.[57]

CRITICISM

A number of educators questioned what Larry Cuban called "the myth of a corporate formula to save the schools."[58] Perhaps the most severe criticism came from Harvard economist Robert B. Reich, who later become Secretary of Labor in President Bill Clinton's administration. Reich was skeptical about the sincerity of corporate America in school reform. He perceived a "pattern of neglect" in corporate giving to public schooling as compared to donations to higher education. "A few corporations take commendably active roles," he declared, "but the vast majority remain on the sidelines."[59] Reich observed that corporate giving to education "has been declining the past five years," and most of the money "flows to the nation's elite colleges."[60] Another educational analyst, George Kaplan, confirmed that "many critics are unimpressed" by corporate giving, noting that in 1990 American businesses "contributed more than $1.73 billion to higher education compared to $264 million for elementary and secondary public education."[61]

Reich pointed out that U.S. corporations seek tax breaks and subsidies in the localities. These considerations undermine public education as they weaken the tax base necessary for supporting public schooling. Most important, Reich questioned the policies of corporate America in employing cheap immigrant labor as contrary to the aims of school reform. "American corporations increasingly are finding skilled workers they need outside the United States," he charged, "and hiring them at a fraction of what they would pay in America."[62] For Reich, this practice goes against business's goal of seeking to improve the educational level of American workers. Indeed, President Bush's 1990 Economic Report sanctioned this business practice. According to the report, the "rising demand for skilled workers" can be ameliorated "by increasing quota limits for potential immigrants with higher levels of basic and specific skills."[63] In short, "the nation can achieve even greater benefits from immigration."[64]

PRIVATIZATION

Business involvement in financial support of public school partnerships and compacts pales by comparison with corporate America's move to enter the educational field with for-profit schools. The idea of running schools for a profit collides with the democratic nature of education. Nevertheless, the fledgling movement for the profit schools had its champions. Writing in the *American School Board Journal*, Marilee C. Rist proclaimed that "a powerful idea is gaining currency in public education these days called privatization."[65]

Privatization emerged as a viable alternative with the rise of choice in public education. The concept of choice has two main meanings: public school choice, whereby a student chooses any public school he or she desires; and private school choice (vouchers), whereby a student chooses any public, private, or parochial school he or she desires. Both ideas had large constituencies in the 1980s and early 1990s. The idea of choice in the voucher version was first promulgated in this country by the conservative Nobel-Prize-winning economist Milton Friedman in the 1960s. A voucher system had been in place in some European countries such as Holland and Denmark. According to Friedman, public education is a monopoly, freed from the constraints of market competition, and it has failed educationally. Friedman argued for a public education system that would receive federal monies in the form of vouchers that would permit students to attend any school they desired, including private schools. Thus, he contended, schools would have to be successful in order to compete for students. In short, this was the law of the marketplace as applied to public education.

The voucher plan gained powerful supporters. An early advocate of vouchers, President Ronald Reagan floated a plan that was rebuffed by Congress. President Bush also became a convert and proclaimed private school choice as crucial to his strategy for excellence reform. However, President Clinton would advocate solely public school choice.

Perhaps the key document in the debate over choice was John E. Chubb and Terry M. Moe's seminal book *Politics, Markets and American Schools*, published in 1991. The authors made the strongest case for private school choice. In a "proposal for reform" they concluded that: "Of all the sundry reforms that attract attention, only choice has the capacity to address America's educational problems ....[W]e think reformers would do well to entertain the notion that choice *is* a panacea ....It has the capacity *all by itself* to bring about the kind of transformation that, for years, reformers have been seeking to engineer in myriad other ways."[66] Chubb and Moe acknowledged that school reform would not have "burst back into the political scene with full force" had it not been for "an essentially unrelated crisis ... in the sphere of economics."[67]

Moreover, they pointed out that "in response to this crisis . . . the business community mobilized their formidable political resources."[68]

The Chubb-Moe analysis departed from conventional arguments for opening up public education to private schools. They added the variable of school governance to other key factors that correlate with student achievement such as family background and school financial resources. Chubb and Moe considered private schooling as the best means to achieve effective school governance because of market competition.

Indeed, the authors challenged the very notion of democratic education as promulgated by John Dewey. For Chubb and Moe, the "democratic institutions by which American public education has been governed . . . appear to be incompatible with effective schooling."[69] And since they concluded that "the schools are failing in their core academic mission," they argued that one must look to the market-oriented private schools as the only credible alternative for school reform.[70] Their sole reservation was that most choice plans relied on existing schools rather than "free[ing] up the supply side" and encouraging "the emergence of new and different types of schools."[71]

Given the Chubb-Moe paradigm, it was inevitable that corporate America would enter the business of establishing schools for profit. The concept of choice/vouchers gave impetus to the fledgling privatization movement. Advocates of privatization contended that American business could provide schools that would raise student achievement and be cost-effective in the bargain. These advocates pointed to a number of school functions that have already been privatized in many school districts, such as transportation, dining, and janitorial services.

On the other hand, critics maintained that privatization goes against the very nature and responsibility of American public education. "The market doesn't care about providing public service," Arnold Ferge of the National Parents and Taxpayers Association charged, "it cares about making money."[72] Further, he observed that American business competes by "providing the least expensive product at the cheapest price" which may not be in the best interests of public school students.[73] In 1991, the National Education Association passed a resolution condemning the "attempts by private corporations . . . to establish schools for profit."[74] The NEA was concerned that "if profit becomes the motive, the children become secondary."[75]

Perhaps the boldest privatization plan was the Edison Project. In 1991, Chris Whittle, a marketing executive with no educational experience, launched a plan to create 200 for-profit schools by the fall of 1996. Whittle's only previous educational foray was in developing a news television program that schools could adopt, Channel One, which carried business advertisements. Whittle's schools sought to enroll some 150,000 students from the ages of 6 months to 6 years. By the year 2010 Whittle hoped to have 2 million students in his schools.[76] Whittle hoped that the schools would be both academically successful and cost-effective. Tuition would be $5,500 per year, approximately the national average for the cost of public education. Whittle would trim teacher costs by increasing the number of teacher aides and volunteers in the classroom, using computerized instruction, and having students do much of the custodial work.[77] Students who could not afford to attend private schools would be eligible for scholarships. Whittle had set aside 20 percent of the student body for scholarship students. However, the ratio would depend on the location of the school. Whereas suburban students may have been be limited to 1 percent of the scholarships, students from urban areas would probably have had more scholarships. For Jonathan Kozol, this admissions criterion was "guaranteeing segregated schooling."[78]

The Edison Project was conceived with school reform in mind. Whittle named it after the great inventor Thomas Edison as a symbol of school reform: "We need a complete redesign of the way we teach our children. This means we cannot begin with the system we now have. When Edison invented electric illumination, he didn't tinker with candles to make them burn better. Instead, he created something brilliantly new: the light bulb."[79]

Whittle obtained funding for the Edison Project from private industry. The media conglomerate Time Warner contributed 38 percent of the stock and Whittle raised $60 million for the project.[80] He assembled a team of "inventors" from business, education, and science among other sectors of society to redesign the American school. Prominent on this team were John C. Chubb, one of the seven-member design team, and consultant Chester E. Finn, Jr., former Assistant Secretary of Education for Research in the Reagan administration. Heading up the Edison Project was former president of Yale University Benno Schmidt.[81] After two years the Edison Project had to be amended. Unable to obtain the $2.5 billion funding for his first 100 schools, Whittle scrapped the idea of building new school plants and reverted to using existing school facilities.[82]

The Edison Project elicited a chorus of skeptics. One state superintendent dubbed the Edison Project "McSchool."[83] For American Federation of Teachers (AFT) president Albert Shanker, there was no global precedent for a chain of private schools: "But among other industrialized countries all over the world . . . we find no example of a country that has entrusted the education of its children to a private system. Instead, they all have fine public systems. There is no reason we should not have one too."[84] Moreover, one think tank analyst questioned whether the Edison Project would be financially viable. "The likelihood of turning a profit is absolutely zero," observed Dennis P. Doyle of the Hudson Institute, "there is absolutely no history of it in the thousand years of education."[85]

Education Alternatives Inc., created in 1991, has operated public schools contracted out by the Baltimore, Los Angeles, and Miami–Dade County systems. The for-profit school firm signed a five-year contract with the Baltimore school board nine public schools in the inner city, with the caveat that the school board could cancel at any time. In the $28 million dollar contract with Baltimore, Education Alternatives hoped to reduce operating expenses by 25 percent and make a profit of 5 percent.[86] Education Alternatives also signed a five-year contract in 1990 with the Dade County school district in Florida to operate one elementary school. Under the $1.2 million contract, Education Alternatives promised to reduce student-teacher ratios through increased use of technology.

After two years, the Baltimore project reported some positive results. Graffiti, crack vials, and other signs of alienation disappeared. A shortage of textbooks was remedied, and the school plant operations problems such as bad plumbing were alleviated. Most important, preliminary test scores in such subjects as reading and math showed gains. The 4,800 students advanced nearly a year in academic achievement during a three-month period.[87] This modest success was attributed to a curriculum that involved greater individualized learning. Teachers were retrained and the number of teacher aides increased to allow for the individualized instruction. The schools were able to obtain a ratio of one helper to four students.[88] This enabled the teachers to account for the different learning styles of pupils.

Equally important, Education Alternatives turned a modest profit. This was accomplished mainly by lowering teacher salaries as well as those of teacher aides and school custodians. This elicited criticism from teacher unions that the privateers were mere "hucksters."[89] Nonetheless, other companies, such as Sylvan Learning Systems, Inc., have become interested in privatization.

The drive for privatization of government services received a boost from the Reason Foundation, a private California foundation that monitors privatization. The foundation publishes how-to-privatize guides and prides itself as the country's leading public policy think tank in the area of privatization. A 1993 guide, *Making Schools Work: Contracting Options for Better Management*, "presents school administrators with a survey of public school practices that involve private-sector providers."[90] Written by Janet R. Beales and John O'Leary, policy analysts with the foundation, the guide gives an overview of how school administrators may contract for both support and core services. Under support services, options are presented on how school districts may buy from private firms services that would manage pupil transportation, food services, janitorial management, and school facilities—the latter involving school construction. Under core services, the authors offer strategies for school administrators to privately manage schools, offer instruction, and design curriculum.

Beales and O'Leary cite examples of for-profit companies in the management, instruction, and curriculum of schools. The instructional strategies range from programs for at-risk students operated by Ombudsman Educational Services, remediation tutoring by Sylvan Learning Systems, science teaching by Science Encounters and Discovering Science, and foreign language teaching by Dialogos International Corporation. In curriculum, the examples stress computer-based curriculum such as that provided by Josten.

Most important, the creation of "charter schools" in a number of states permit public school districts to be exempt from traditional regulations allowing for various degrees of privatization. For Beales and O'Leary, public school systems are "monopolies" that are "inherently inefficient."[91] Consequently, they concluded that "the great value of public-private partnerships and contracting arrangements is that they harness competitive efficiencies to the benefit of student welfare."[92]

Will privatization become a major force in American education? Beales is cautiously optimistic. "Privatization certainly could gain a firm stronghold," she states, "as school boards become more comfortable with the contracting of support services over conventional business operations, we may see more contracting out of entire public schools to private industry."[93]

"THE FORGOTTEN HALF"

Some economists consider that the failure of American schools is with those 50 percent of high school graduates who do not attend college—dubbed by some analysts as "the forgotten half." For example, economist Lester G. Thurow pointed to the German apprenticeship program as the global model for industrialized nations. This apprenticeship program, jointly administered by industry and the schools, Thurow argued, "constitutes the key ingredient in German economic success."[94] Thurow observed that "the Germans are not the best educated at the top, nor are they the best educated at the bottom."[95] But he observed that "they are the world's very best over a broad range of middle, noncollege skills."[96] And it is this skilled workforce that has made the German economy one of the world's best.

The German apprenticeship program consists of training on a two-tier level. First, youngsters at age 15 to 16 train in specific skills for three years. They must pass written examinations in order to be certified as a journeyman in the field. Second, those wishing to operate a small business must take an additional three years of schooling in such subjects as management, law, and technology. Again, they must pass a written examination to qualify as masters in their skill. Thurow concluded that this system "is the envy of the rest of the world."[97]

Other countries have attempted to replicate this model. France has induced industry to provide apprenticeship training by rebating a 1 percent sale tax to firms that initiate such programs.[98] Unfortunately, according to Thurow, the United States is "unique among industrialized countries" in not having "an organized postsecondary education" for the forgotten half.[99]

A number of educators have grappled with the problem. In 1988, the William T. Grant Foundation Commission on Work, Family and Citizenship completed a study entitled "The Forgotten Half: Pathways to Success for America's Youth and Young Families." The report graphically portrayed the lack of national attention to those high school graduates not destined for college. Nevertheless, the commission's recommendations were a far cry from those envisioned by Thurow. The commission suggested increased funding for programs already in place as well as new programs. The commission recommended an additional $5 billion a year for ten years for "effective existing programs such as Head Start" and an added $250 million for five years to states for "demonstration grants" to create a "coordinated and comprehensive program for postsecondary training and education."[100] The commission also applauded "the promising local compacts" between business and the schools.[101]

President Clinton took a first step in solving the problem. His administration introduced legislation, *Goals 2000: Educate America Act*, that among other things would "stimulate the development of a voluntary national system of skill standards and certification to serve as the cornerstone of the national strategy to enhance workforce skills."[102] For that purpose a National Skills Standards Board would be created composed of twenty-eight members including the Secretaries of Labor, Education, and Commerce; eight representatives from industry; eight from labor; and eight from education, each serving four-year terms. This board would receive $15 million in 1994 and "such sums as may be necessary for each of fiscal years 1995 through 1999."[103] In addition the Departments of Education and Labor would establish a $270 million program to guide the transition from school to work.[104] The bill passed the House of Representatives by a 307-188 vote with strong bipartisan support.[105]

CONCLUSION

The ultimate question is: Should business be involved in American public education? For Joel Spring, the answer is no. For him, the problem lies with "the short range goals of business," which in times of economic stress result in pressure on the public schools to produce "more scientists and engineers to win the technological race."[106] Spring predicted that "if current trends continue, then public schools will primarily serve the interests of business and politicians."[107] But Spring's greatest reservations were with the trend toward privatization: "One possible direction for the schools is privatization. . . . The Edison Project by the Whittle Corporation to franchise schools may foreshadow a future in which schools will be marketed in a manner similar to the way that fast food chains are marketed. If this is the future, then it seems very unlikely that schools will promote the tenets of a free society."[108]

Privatization strikes at the nature of American public education. Whereas public schooling has been based on a moral responsibility, privatization has as its major goal making a profit. With a policy of choice/vouchers, the United States might accelerate its tracked system of urban and suburban schools. There is evidence that choice plans increasingly segregate at-risk (read "minority") and handicapped students.[109] In short, the drift toward privatization marks the excellence reform movement repudiating the tradition of concern for the poor in the progressive and equity reform movements.

Moreover, there is the question of equal funding. By giving money to select districts, other school districts, not as fortunate, suffer by comparison. Referring to this special treatment, Shanker scored the takeover of the Chelsea School Board by Boston University. President John Silber promised a "model of school reform across the nation,"[110] but in order to fulfill that promise BU had to raise added funds from business and foundations. "There should be public concern," Shanker asked, over "the issue of money."[111] Shanker captured the dilemma: "If only BU can get the money, what happens when BU gets out of the picture . . . .How do grants or gifts get the district into solid financial shape after the 'soft' money disappears?"[112]

Nevertheless, there have been positive aspects of the business-schools relationship. The compact model, despite its implementation problems, serves a useful purpose. By guaranteeing entry-level positions to high school graduates, business has given the right kind of financial support.

Perhaps the greatest challenge of corporate America will be in developing a training program for the forgotten half who do not attend college, a program in the manner of the European nations. This may prove to be business's most lasting contribution. Until then, the messianic zeal of corporate America to "save the schools" may be more shouting than substance.

NOTES

1. Benjamin M. Friedman, *Day of Reckoning: The Consequences of American Economic Policy Under Reagan and After* (New York: Random House, 1988), p. 4.

2. *Ibid.*, p. 51.

3. *New York Times*, March 4, 1991, p. 1.

4. National Commission on Excellence in Education, *A Nation at Risk: The Imperative for Educational Reform* (Washington, D.C.: U.S. Department of Education, 1983), p. 5.

5. *Ibid.*, pp. 6–7.

6. Northwest Regional Exchange, "The National Report on Education: A Comparative Analysis," in *The Great School Debates*, edited by Beatrice Gross and Ronald Gross (New York: Simon and Schuster, 1985), p. 56.

7. *Ibid.*, p. 66.

8. George Kaplan, "Scapegoating the Schools," in *Voices from the Field*, edited by Samuel Halperin (Washington, D.C.: William T. Grant and Foundation Commission on Work, Family and Citizenship, Institute for Educational Leadership, 1991), p. 11.

9. Larry Cuban, "The Corporate Myth of Reforming Public Schools," *Phi Delta Kappan*, October 1992, p. 159.

10. *Ibid.*

11. Michael Timpane, "Business Has Rediscovered the Public Schools," *Phi Delta Kappan*, February 1984, p. 389.

12. *Ibid.*, p. 392.

13. George Kaplan, "The Changing Look of Education's Policy Networks," *Phi Delta Kappan*, May 1992, p. 667.

14. *New York Times*, November 6, 1993, p. A14.

15. *New York Times*, November 19, 1993, p. A16.

16. *Ibid.*

17. Marilee C. Rist, "Business Takes Action in School Reform," *The Education Digest*, November 1990, p. 47.

18. Jessica Skelly von Brachel, "How Business Helps the Schools," *Fortune*, October 21, 1991, p. 161.

19. *Ibid.*

20. *Ibid.*

21. U.S. Department of Education, *America 2000: An Education Strategy* (Washington, D.C.: U.S. Government Printing Office, April 18, 1991), p. 15.

22. *Ibid.*, pp. 16–17.

23. *Ibid.*, p. 16.

24. *Ibid.*

25. Michael Kirst, "Toward a Focused Research Agenda," in *Voices from the Field*, edited by Samuel Halperin (Washington, D.C.: William T. Grant Foundation Commission on Work, Family and Citizenship, 1991), p. 38.

26. *Ibid.*

27. *Ibid.*

28. Diane Ravitch, *The Troubled Crusade: American Education 1945–1980*, (New York: Basic Books, 1983), p. 257.

29. *Ibid.*, p. 250.

30. *Ibid.*, p. 261.

31. *Ibid.*, p. 260.

32. Rist, "Business Takes Action," p. 47.

33. "The Boston Compact Fosters City-wide Collaboration," *Educational Record*, Fall 1987/Winter 1988, p. 51.

34. *Ibid.*

35. *Ibid.*

36. Rist, "Business Takes Action," p. 48.

37. *Ibid.*, p. 50.

38. National Alliance for Business, *The Compact Project: Final Report* (Washington, D.C.: National Alliance for Business, 1991), p. 1.

39. *Ibid.*, p. 23.

40. *Ibid.*, p. 2.

41. *Ibid.*, p. 4.

42. Donald M. Clark, "School/Business Partnerships Are Too Much Talk and Not Enough Performance," *The American School Board Journal*, August 1988, p. 33.

43. *Ibid.*

44. Robert E. Slavin, "IBM's Writing to Read: Is It Right for Reading?" *Phi Delta Kappan*, November 1990, p. 214.

45. *Ibid.*, p. 215.

46. *Ibid.*, p. 216.

47. *Ibid.*

48. *Ibid.*

49. Ann-Carol Banton Holley, *A Comparative Study of the Effects of Two Urban Kindergarten Beginning Reading Programs on Student Oral Reading Performance and Attitudes Toward Reading*, Ph.D. dissertation (Norfolk, Va.: Old Dominion University, 1988), p. 119.

50. *Ibid.*, p. 2.

51. Interview with Ann-Carol Banton Holley, Norfolk, Va., September 28, 1993.

52. Association for Supervision and Curriculum, "Guidelines for Business Involvement in the Schools," *Educational Leadership*, December 1989/January 1990, p. 84.

53. *Ibid.*

54. *Ibid.*

55. *Ibid.*

56. *Ibid.*

57. *Ibid.*

58. Cuban, "The Corporate Myth," p. 159.

59. Robert B. Reich, "Education Reform, Don't Count on Business," *Harper's Magazine*, September 1992, p. 26.

60. *Ibid.*

61. Kaplan, "The Changing Look of Education," p. 668.

62. Reich, "Education Reform," p. 27.

63. *Ibid.*

64. *Ibid.*

65. Marilee C. Rist, "Education, Inc.," *The American School Board Journal*, September 1991, p. 24.

66. John E. Chubb and Terry M. Moe, *Politics, Markets and American Schools* (Washington, D.C.: The Brookings Institution, 1990), pp. 216–217.

67. *Ibid.*, p. 9.

68. *Ibid.*

69. *Ibid.*, p. 2.

70. *Ibid.*, p. 1.
71. *Ibid.*, p. 207.
72. Rist, "Education, Inc." p. 29.
73. *Ibid.*
74. *Ibid.*
75. *Ibid.*
76. Marilee C. Rist, "Here Comes 'McSchool,' " *The American School Board Journal*, September 1991, p. 30.
77. Jonathan Kozol, "Whittle and the Privateers," *The Nation*, September 21, 1992, p. 274.
78. *Ibid.*
79. Albert Shanker, "Edison's Candle," *New York Times*, August 29, 1993, p. E7.
80. Kozol, "Whittle and the Privateers," p. 274.
81. *Ibid.*, p. 277.
82. Rist, "Here Comes 'McSchool,' " p. 30.
83. *Ibid.*
84. Shanker, "Edison's Candle," p. E7.
85. Rist, "Here Comes 'McSchool,' " p. 31.
86. Janet R. Beales and John O'Leary, *Making Schools Work: Contracting Options for Better Management* (Los Angeles: Reason Foundation, November 1993), p. 19.
87. *New York Times*, October 6, 1993, p. B10.
88. *Ibid.*
89. *Ibid.*
90. Beales and O'Leary, *Making Schools Work*, p. 102.
91. *Ibid.*, p. 28.
92. *Ibid.*
93. Interview with Janet R. Beales, Education Policy Analyst, Reason Foundation, Los Angeles, Calif., October 13, 1993 (telephone).
94. Lester G. Thurow, *Head to Head: The Coming Economic Battle Among Japan, Europe, and America* (New York: William Morrow and Co., 1992), p. 55.
95. *Ibid.*
96. *Ibid.*
97. *Ibid.*, p. 275.
98. *Ibid.*
99. *Ibid.*
100. William T. Grant Foundation Commission on Work, Family and Citizenship, "The Forgotten Half: Pathways to Success for America's Youth and Young Families," *Phi Delta Kappan*, December 1988, pp. 288–289.
101. *Ibid.*, p. 288.
102. U.S. Department of Education, *Goals 2000: Educate America Act* (Washington, D.C.: U.S. Government Printing Office, October 1993), p. 70.
103. *Ibid.*, p. 81.
104. *New York Times*, April 22, 1993, p. A20.
105. *Virginian Ledger-Star*, October 14, 1993, p. 1.
106. Joel Spring, *Conflict of Interests: The Politics of American Education* (White Plains, N.Y.: Longman, 1993), p. 220.
107. *Ibid.*, p. 224.

108. *Ibid.*

109. Donald R. Moore and Suzanne Davenport, *School Choice: The New and Improved Sorting Machine* (Chicago: Designs for Change, February 1989).

110. Albert Shanker, "Chelsea Three Years Later," *New York Times*, October 4, 1993, p. E7.

111. Albert Shanker, "Chelsea Plan Needs Scrutiny," *New York Times*, November 27, 1988, p. E7.

112. *Ibid.*

CHAPTER SEVEN

THE SCHOOL CULTURE WARS

A distinctive feature of excellence reform was the battle over school curriculum. Combatants in the culture wars, seeking to define the soul of American schooling, were divided into three camps. The Western traditionalists argued that the United States possessed a common culture that was derived from European origins. The Afrocentrists declared the need for school curricula that reflected the African origins of the African-American experience. Establishing a middle group were varying multiculturalists, who emphasized both a Eurocentric and a multicultural emphasis.

The Western traditionalists won the battle in the media and in the mind of the general public. Championed by such powerful establishment figures as Diane Ravitch, Arthur Schlesinger, Jr., and Albert Shanker—with a key study by Virginia professor E. D. Hirsch, Jr.—they sought a counterreform. Nonetheless, the quieter arguments of the multiculturalists won the day in school and college curricula. The counterreform of the Western traditionalists marked the end of what Henry Luce called the American Century. As U.S. economic influence dwindled globally, and as the world shrank in an age of mass communications, the effort by the Western traditionalists to establish a common American culture constituted a rear guard action. Moreover, as the multiculturalists were happy to point out, national demographics were also changing. Immigration had been drastically restricted for Europeans since 1924, but with the reform of 1965 that opened up Asian migration, some sociologists estimated that within a generation nearly half of U.S. school children would be black, Hispanic, or Asian.[1] The question of a common national culture was, then, never more urgent.

A Nation at Risk officially initiated the debate over a common culture. This study by the National Commission on Excellence in Education recommended a core curriculum in schools that would comprise "five new basics": English, mathematics, social studies, science, and computer science.[2] Eight years later, President George Bush's *America 2000* proposed national standards and voluntary national tests in core subjects: English, mathematics, science, history, and geography.[3] A core curriculum with national standards and national testing implied a national curriculum. Polls indicated that the American public favored a national curriculum. In anticipation of a movement toward a national curriculum, the debate over a common American culture erupted.

THE WESTERN TRADITIONALISTS

E. D. Hirsch, Jr.

The key document in the culture wars representing the Western traditionalists' point of view was E. D. Hirsch, Jr.'s 1987 book *Cultural Literacy: What Every American Needs to Know*, which became a national best seller. The book followed by seven years Molefi Kete Asante's extension of the civil rights agenda in his book *Afrocentricity*. Hirsch correctly established the thrust of the Western traditionalists by calling his effort "the counter-reform of the 1980's to the legacy of the social 1960's."[4] Hirsch argued for a common American culture after two decades of national focus on ethnicity and diversity.

The Civil Rights Movement redirected the emphasis on ethnicity. From the progressive era to the 1960s, the focus was on the assimilation of white European ethnics. The Civil Rights Movement reawakened the concern with difference. Indeed, the Black Power phase carried ethnicity to its logical conclusion: Black Power asked "Who am I?" The question of identity dominated American black concerns and spread to other groups. Feminism was an offshoot of the Civil Rights Movement as women saw the need to redefine themselves. Descendants of ethnic Europeans rediscovered their ancestry. Scholars mined the field. Black, Latino, women's, and ethnic studies departments and programs were created at U.S. universities. Academic journals were devoted to these new "fields." The homogenized and sanitized American character, which was the model for ethnic Europeans to emulate in the progressive era, was replaced by the multicultural American character.

It was against this mosaic that Hirsch and his colleagues would establish their rear guard action. Hirsch proposed his "counterreform" to do no less than move schools "to a more traditional curriculum."[5] There was an economic matrix to Hirsch's call. On the first page of *Cultural Literacy*, he spoke of the educational success of the homogeneous society of the United States' chief economic competitor: "Much of Japan's industrial efficiency has been credited to its almost universally high level of literacy."[6] There was an urgency to Hirsch's plea for a common culture. He noted that, "American business leaders have become alarmed by the lack of communication skills in the young people they employ."[7]

In order to successfully launch his counterreformation, Hirsch first found that he had to challenge the legacy of progressive education. Progressive education stressed natural development, process, and critical thinking goals that ran counter to Hirsch's content-based curricula. For Hirsch, the fault with U.S. education lay with the theories of Jean Jacques Rousseau whose "ideas influenced the educational conceptions of John Dewey, the writer who has most deeply affected American educational history and practice."[8] Hirsch charged that Dewey advocated "the content-neutral curriculum" for the national development of young children.[9] For Hirsch, "Dewey was deeply mistaken."[10]

Hirsch offered instead the content-specific curriculum grounded in the Western tradition. He did not define precisely what he meant by cultural literacy. Rather, he defined it as a vague method of acquiring "shared knowledge" that would enable one to "possess the basic information needed to thrive in the modern world."[11] On close inspection, that definition translates into a national culture emanating from the Eurocentric tradition:

But in a diverse society, who has the right to define nationwide requirements? . . . Shall we aim for the gradual assimilation of all into one national culture, or shall we honor and preserve the diverse cultures implicit in our hyper-nations? . . .

If we had to make a choice between the one and the *many*, most Americans would choose the principle of unity, since we cannot function as a nation without it. . . .

It is for the Amish to decide what Amish traditions are, but it is for all of us to decide collectively what our traditions are, to decide what "American" means on the other side of the hyphen in Italo-American or Asian-American. What national values and traditions really belong to cultural literacy?[12]

One school administrator perceived the attraction and the pitfalls of the idea of a common culture. Curriculum specialist Benjamin Troutman conceded "the fundamental, compelling power" of cultural literacy "in this age of fragmentation" since "it offers unification and coherence."[13] By the same token, however, Troutman observed that "any established canon for curriculum, although unifying, is also exclusionary."[14]

Hirsch fleshed out his lexicon on essential "shared information" in sixty-three pages of short identifications. These items chiefly reflect Western accomplishments and are tilted toward a white, male, Eurocentric culture. Critics have charged that they are a version of a "Trivial Pursuit" parlor game that misinterprets the nature of education.

Most important, Hirsch's key assumption that a national culture is, by and large, immutable is open to question. Whereas Hirsch would admit to slight revisions to a core culture, historians perceive revision that is less linear. History may recede as well as proceed; and progress sometimes is cataclysmic rather than in an unbroken even line. America's entry into world literature in the 1920s subsumed the literature that preceded it. Similarly, America's entry into the international art world, with abstract expressionism, was a cataclysmic event that Hirsch's linear model fails to grasp. Correspondingly, the civil rights and feminist movements were not simply historical events; they both transformed and redirected U.S. history.

Hirsch operationalized his ideas. In 1986, he founded the Core Knowledge Foundation, a not-for-profit organization offering his core curricula to schools. These core curricula comprised a sequence from the first to the sixth grade, which would account for half of a school's curriculum. The core curricula were content specific, requiring rote learning to assimilate the knowledge. As of 1993, 100 schools in 29 states used Hirsch's core curricula.[15]

Hirsch referred to his foundation's efforts as a "Core Knowledge Movement."[16] In his promotional literature, he claimed that "*the most experienced and fully committed* Core Knowledge schools are reporting: increased professional collaboration; improved standardized test scores; tremendous student and parent enthusiasm" (emphasis added).[17] Hirsch trumpeted the success of one inner city school in a *New York Times* op-ed piece. According to Hirsch, P.S. 67 in the South Bronx had a 13.5 percent increase in reading scores. He attributed much of that success to the fact that his core curriculum avoided "learning to learn skills, critical thinking skills and problem skills"—the essence of progressive education—for content-specific "core knowledge."[18]

Moreover, Hirsch advertised his Core Knowledge curriculum as blending with the thrust of the excellence reform movement. "Whatever the national standards," Hirsch maintained, "schools using CORE Knowledge can be confident that their programs will meet or exceed those standards."[19] Added to this promotional literature was an endorsement from Albert Shanker. For Shanker, Core Knowledge established "clear expectations for the kids and their teachers" and "has a curriculum that specifies a certain body of core knowledge."[20]

The Core Knowledge sequence included six texts by Hirsch for each respective grade. These texts were designed to provide a "specific sequence of core knowledge that young Americans should, at a minimum, learn."[21] Hirsch claimed that core knowledge constituted the "necessary step in developing a first rate educational system in the United States."[22]

One critic found the materials not only "drab" and not likely "to charm or interest students" but "stupid and dangerous."[23] Teacher activist Herbert Kohl worried that the Core Knowledge curriculum promoted the status quo, glossing over a need for "fundamental economic and social change."[24] He concluded that: "In practice, the core curriculum enshrines the values of the people who determine it as universal standards of excellence. Nazi Germany had a core curriculum, after all, as did the Stalinist Soviet Union."[25] Nevertheless, Kohl found positive value in Hirsch's reassessment of progressive education and the need for some content-specific curricula. Kohl opted for a combination whereby "process and content" become "merged into a thoughtful and critical pedagogy."[26]

Core Knowledge curriculum is based on rote learning, reverting to the education that the progressives revolted against. In this sense much of the excellence reform movement, with its emphasis on basics, standards, and core curricula, is retrograde.

Diane Ravitch

One of the most influential advocates for a common American culture was Diane Ravitch. Ravitch was a scholar activist who not only took an active role in the New York State and California curriculum battles, but she assumed the leadership in excellence reform, succeeding Chester E. Finn, Jr., as Assistant Secretary of Education for Research in the Bush administration.

In *Cultural Literacy*, Hirsch acknowledged his debt to Ravitch. According to Hirsch, "The single greatest impetus to writing this book came from Diane Ravitch, who said simply that I ought to write a book, that I ought to call it *Cultural Literacy*—and that I ought to get it out as soon as possible."[27]

The target of the Western traditionalists was the other extreme: Afrocentric curricula. And Diane Ravitch levied her strongest criticism at the Afrocentrists. She correctly observed that the Afrocentric curriculum "has its intellectual roots in the ideology of . . . the black nationalist movement."[28] It was part of "the ethnic revival of the 1960's" that received operational definition in the community control movement.[29] However, for Ravitch, ethnocentrism was a "bad idea whose time has come."[30]

Instead, Ravitch made a plea for a "common culture that is multicultural . . . paradoxical thought it may seem."[31] For Ravitch, the accent was on a common culture rooted in the Western tradition. She advocated the principle of " 'E Pluribus Unum'—the one common culture weaving the strands of the many separate cultures."[32] If America were to fail on that ideal, she would abandon public schooling. Without a common U.S. culture in school curricula, she charged, "we have . . . no reason to support public education."[33] Consequently, one can understand Ravitch's later position, promoting school vouchers.

Ravitch questioned the positive self-esteem that might result from Afrocentric curricula. "The danger of this remedy," she maintained, "is that it will detract from the real needs of the schools."[34] For Ravitch, the "real needs" were traditional ones: "well-educated and well-paid teachers, small classes, good materials, encouragement at home and school, summer academic programs, protection from drugs and crime that ravage their neighborhoods, and higher expectations of satisfying careers upon graduation."[35]

Ravitch accompanied Hirsch's *Cultural Literacy* with a reader on democracy. In *The Democracy Reader*, Ravitch and her co-author Abigail Thernstrom maintained that "we can say with assurance . . . that democracy is the best form of government yet devised."[36] *The Democracy Reader* consists of a compendium of selected writings generally reflecting the Western tradition. In those cases where non-Western writers are included, they comprise a group that is, for the most part, anticommunist. There are no articles from dissenters from right-wing nations such as those that exist in Latin America. It is a skewed sample from a writer who, ironically, opposed the extension of democratic rights in schools to poor and minority parents in the community control struggle.

The first section of *The Democracy Reader* represents "classical and European thought."[37] All of the selections are from white, male Europeans. The second section deals with "the American experience."[38] Of the authors represented, only two are black: Martin Luther King, Jr., and Frederick Douglass. There are no Black Power activists represented, such as Malcolm X. Only one woman is represented in the American section: Susan B. Anthony. Omitted are recent femininist authors. Only one selection is from Native Americans—the declaration from the Seneca Indians—and none from the leaders of the American Indian Movement of the 1970s. There are five entries by Thomas Jefferson, three by Abraham Lincoln, two by Martin Luther King, Jr., and one by conservative philosopher Sidney Hook, a former disciple of John Dewey. There is none by Dewey, nor are any members of American labor or radical groups represented. The third section on "contemporary international democratic ideas" does not fare any better. Of the fifty-two entries, most favor anticommunist dissidents. These include five Soviet writers, five Polish, three Chinese, two Romanian, two Cuban, one Hungarian, and one Czechoslovakian. Understandably, *The Democracy Reader* was blessed by Albert Shanker and the American Federation of Teachers. Ravitch and Thernstrom noted that they "received encouragement from the American Federation of Teachers, which became convinced of the need for a comprehensive collection of documents about democracy on the part of free teachers unions in nations struggling to achieve democracy."[39]

Arthur Schlesinger, Jr. *Amu̶rican → multicultural*

Another powerful advocate of the Western tradition was the historian Arthur Schlesinger, Jr., whose polemic *The Disuniting of America: Reflections on a Multicultural Society* also became a national best seller. Schlesinger's book reflected his involvement in the controversial social studies revisions in New York State. In his rejoinder, Schlesinger argued that revived ethnicity threatened to dissolve the fragile bond of a common American culture. Schlesinger argued that "the vision of America as melted into one people prevailed through most of the two centuries of the history of the United States."[40] Most important, he concluded that the melting pot was the result of the public schools being "the great instrument of assimilation and the great means of forming an American identity."[41]

Schlesinger was one of many consensus historians who rose to prominence after World War II. They were the dominant historical school, stressing U.S. history as essentially a coming together of various interest groups around a common good, a consensus of a linear American progress. The assumptions of the consensus historians came under severe challenge from the revisionists, who grew up in the shadow of the civil rights and anti-war movements. The revisionists had as their guiding historical principle confrontation, rather than consensus, and questioned the consensus historians' assumption of linear historical progress. In education they accumulated a great deal of evidence, through new methodologies, that nineteenth- and twentieth-century public schools had a darker side. Michael Katz echoed the sentiment of his revisionist colleagues by branding the common school at the time of the European immigration as not only intent on "blurring cultural distinctiveness" but having a "racist implication" that "scarred the origins of public education."[42] Indeed, Schlesinger admitted that his German father had queried his grandfather "why the school books portrayed England as the one and only mother country."[43] Schlesinger concluded that U.S. history was "written in the interests of white Anglo-Saxon Protestant males."[44] Nevertheless, Schlesinger retreated from this example to hold that the "anglocentric domination of school books was based *in part* on unassailable facts" (emphasis added).[45]

Moreover, there was the contrary evidence of Catholic education. Although little has been written on Catholic education, what scholarly studies exist indicate that the Catholic schools preserved not only their religious orientation but their cultures as well. The Catholic parochial schools were created in 1884 as a response to the largely Anglo dominance of public education that often resulted in anti-Catholic attitudes. In his study of parochial education in Chicago, *The Education of an Urban Minority: Catholics in Chicago 1833–1965*, James W. Sanders showed that Catholics flocked to these parochial schools with the intention to preserve their religion and their ethnicity. As many as eleven ethnically different parochial school subsystems existed in Chicago. They included those for French, German, Polish, and other multilanguage students. (My own experience in Maine in the 1940s confirms Sanders study. There were two systems, one French with the instruction in French and the other for mainly Irish students taught in English.) Sanders concluded that the Chicago parochial schools "allowed the maximum local diversity and as it turns out, each ethnic, cultural, and educational group flourished."[46]

Schlesinger targeted the Afrocentric curricula. He reduced these curricula to "the use of history as therapy" with an avowed intention to raise the self-esteem of minority children.[47] For Schlesinger, such "feel good history" is simply "bad history."[48] Schlesinger argued that "the cult of ethnicity in general and the Afrocentric campaign, in particular, do not bode well for the future of the republic."[49] Afrocentrism was no less than an "attack on the common identity."[50] Moreover, he seriously doubted whether "learning about Africa" would "improve the self-esteem of black children."[51]

In short, Schlesinger upheld the Great Western tradition. "There surely is no reason for western civilization to have guilt trips," he asserted, "laid on it by champions of cultures based on despotism, superstition, tribalism, and fanaticism."[52] One could argue that much of that description applies to the Eurocentric tradition from the Spanish Inquisition to the Holocaust. Former Secretary of Education in the Reagan administration, William J. Bennett, rephrased Schlesinger's beliefs more boldly. Bennett admonished schools and colleges to "defend western civilization . . . because it is good. . . . [W]estern ideas remain still the last, best hope on earth."[53]

Critics pointed out that *The Disuniting of America* was an attempt to discredit not only the Afrocentrists but, in effect, the multiculturalists as well. Michael Bérubé, a professor of English, concluded that: "*Disuniting* . . . isn't really about multiculturalism at all; it's about Afrocentrism as Schlesinger sees it, an extremist Afrocentrism he describes as a cult of ethnicity. . . . [F]ew important books on the subject are as confused as *The Disuniting of America* . . . [which] performs as a licensing text, a document which serves to authorize backlash against multiculturalism."[54]

Other scholars compared the work of the Western traditionalists to a new "neo-nativism" that provoked a "renewed America debate" about "what it means to be an American in the 1990's."[55] They argued that this renewed debate came at a time when millions of immigrants from the

Far East and Latin America were migrating to the United States. And they maintained that the common American culture debate lay at the heart of excellence reform: "Neo-nativists would contain diversity and individualism by a standardized education—by national standards in core subjects, national assessments and a de facto national curriculum."[56]

AFROCENTRISTS

The Western traditionalists focused on a key work published in 1980 entitled simply *Afrocentricity*. The author of that book, Molefi Kete Asante, is chairperson of the Department of African-American Studies at Temple University. He plainly intended his ruminations for a black audience in search of a usable past. Although not specifically concerned with a school curriculum, Asante laid the groundwork for a reconnection of black Americans with both an African-American experience and an African experience. On page one, he advanced the notion that for a formerly enslaved people "Afrocentricity is the centerpiece of human regeneration."[57] He offered a clear definition of Afrocentricity: "Afrocentricity is the belief in the centrality of Africans in post modern history. It is our history, our mythology, our creative motif, and our ethos exemplifying our collective will."[58]

Asante argued that for blacks in America their roots lie in Africa. "The core of our collective being is Africa," he declared, "that is, our awareness of separateness from the Anglo-American experience is a function of our historical moment."[59] Asante maintained that although the Eurocentric linkage claims universality, the alternative doctrine of Afrocentricity reveals the Western tradition to be "only one way to view the world."[60] Asante recommended for black Americans "to begin with African-American history and mythology."[61]

Consequently, he invoked a history that began with the "great prophets," from Booker T. Washington to Malcolm X. For these "great prophets" he had nothing but praise. He found Booker T. Washington to be "one of the most astute black leaders who ever lived"; Marcus Garvey developed a philosophy that "was the most perfect, consistent, and brilliant ideology of liberation in the first half of the 20th century"; Martin Luther King, Jr., promoted "a significant action philosophy"; W.E.B. DuBois stood "at the helm of intellectual and political advancement in the contemporary world"; Elijah Muhammad was "an effective organizer who readily grasped our economic realities"; and Malcolm X was "an activist commentator on the revolutionary road to an Afrocentrist viewpoint."[62]

Asante offered a common black American culture in the grouping of the "great prophets." Unfortunately, in striving to establish a common thread, he blurred differences. In the postmodern wake of the Civil

Rights Movement, many in the African-American community have sought a common front. However, these "great prophets" differed significantly in philosophy and strategy although agreeing on the main aim of eliminating racism.

Beyond the African-American experience, Asante wanted his readers to return to the "cradle of human history" in Africa.[63] Asante sought "an African cultural system" for American blacks.[64]

Asante countered the Western traditionalists in a reply to Diane Ravitch. He argued that "there is no common American culture."[65] Rather, he contended that "to believe in multicultural education is to assume that there are many cultures."[66] However, since there exists "a common American society," he wrote, "this nation is on the path toward a common culture."[67] The key is schooling. "The debate over the curriculum," Asante concluded, "is really over a vision of the future of the United States."[68]

He dismissed the criticism of the Western traditionalists that at the heart of the Afrocentric curriculum was the raising of self-esteem of black children, claiming that no Afrocentric curriculum planner had as his or her "primary aim" to "raise self-esteem."[69] The major purpose, he argued, was to provide the black student with "*accurate* information" that might have a "secondary effect which would result in the adjustment of attitudes of both black and white students."[70]

Asante's strongest argument was that the Western traditionalists were victims of a cultural lag. The emergence of the global village, through telecommunications and inexpensive air travel, had made the rest of the world more accessible. The dominance of foreign economies aided in this newfound emphasis on internationalism. Asante cited this "different reality," which was the consequence of an "accelerating explosion in the world about cultures, histories, and events seldom previously mentioned in American education."[71]

Asante had supporters beyond the African-American community. Joel Spring, a descendent of the Choctaw nation, found that "schools molded on Afrocentric education . . . may be a more realistic approach for dominated groups."[72] Spring gave a resounding "yes" to Afrocentric education as providing greater knowledge for blacks in the United States. Moreover, he believed that "the Afrocentric model is applicable to other dominated groups."[73]

Afrocentrism has interesting parallels with the religious orientation inculcated in Catholic schools. The difference is that one promotes a religiocultural perspective in a *private* school and the other promotes an Afrocentric perspective in a *public* school. One could view the community control movement, with its initial foray at Afrocentrism, as an attempt to convert the American public school system into a quasi-private one.

THE MULTICULTURALISTS

Located somewhere on the spectrum between the Western tradition-alists and the Afrocentrists are the multiculturalists. The multiculturalists occupy a shifting position that does not fall into either extreme camp. Calling themselves "mainstream multiculturalists," a group of scholars including James A. Banks, Carl A. Grant, and Christine Sleeter, among others, have waged a campaign to revise public school curricula with more emphasis on diversity. While the Western traditionalists have won the battle in the minds of the American public and the media, and the Afrocentrists have been clearly on the defensive, the multiculturalists have won the war. Most public schools and universities have revised their curricula to offer more multicultural diversity.

The multiculturalists agree with the Western traditionalists on "the notion of *e pluribus unum*—out of many, one" but differ on "how the *unum* can best be attained."[74] The multiculturalists favor more emphasis on "the nation's ethnic and cultural diversity" than do the Western tra-ditionalists.[75] On the other hand, they distance themselves from the Af-rocentrists by arguing that "multicultural education itself is a thoroughly Western movement."[76] Still, they acknowledge a cultural "debt to people of color and women" so that their multicultural curricula evidence "the discrepancies between the ideals of freedom and equality and the reali-ties of racism and sexism."[77]

The multiculturalists also point to changing demographics as the im-petus of their campaign to include more diversity in public school cur-ricula. They project an increase in minority population such that, within a generation, almost half of all public school students will be black, His-panic, or Asian.[78] Consequently, they contend that multicultural educa-tion, rather than being divisive, will "help a divided nation and society to become more unified."[79] Most important, they are cognizant of the subtle shift in educational policy that has quietly occurred in schools and universities. They cite the 1977 decision by the National Council on Ac-creditation of Teacher Education that included a new standard for ac-crediting colleges of education that "gives evidence of planning for multicultural education in its teaching of curricula."[80] Moreover, text-book companies, which are *de facto* creators of a national curriculum, have commissioned texts to reflect the viewpoints of the multicultural scholars.

CASE STUDY: THE NEW YORK STATE CURRICULUM BATTLE

In 1989, the first major confrontation over school curriculum took place in New York. This controversy generated much antagonism, and, in the end, none of the parties was fully satisfied with the various "compromise" measures proposed for the state.

The controversy began with the appointment of a white liberal, Thomas Sobol, as State Commissioner of Education. An educational reformer, Sobol sought to review New York State curricula and guidelines, partly to offset criticism from minorities about his selection. He appointed a Task Force on Minorities, chaired by the president of the New York chapter of the National Association for the Advancement of Colored People (NAACP), to produce guidelines for a new social studies curriculum. The seventeen-member task force had but one white participant and no historians.

In July of 1989, the task force released its report, entitled *A Curriculum of Inclusion*. The Western traditionalists focused on the first sentence of the report: "African-Americans, Asian-Americans, Puerto Ricans, Latinos and Native Americans have all been the victims of an intellectual and educational oppression that has characterized the culture and institutions of the United States and the European American world for centuries."[81] Moreover, they challenged the report's assertion that the public schools were guilty of a "systematic bias toward European culture" that has "a terrible damaging effect" on minorities, so much so that "large numbers of children of non-European descent are not doing as well as expected."[82]

Ravitch characterized the report as "consistently Europhobic" and that it "repeatedly expresses negative judgments on European Americans and on everything Western and European."[83] Ravitch concluded that students should not be subject to curricula that view "the world through an ethnocentric perspective that rejects or ignores the common culture."[84]

Schlesinger condemned the report as a "reconstruction of American history partly on the merits and partly in response to ethnic pressures."[85] He demeaned the historical value of the social studies curriculum guide as "an intellectual discipline" and regarded it mainly as an attempt at "social and psychological therapy whose primary purpose is to raise the self-esteem of children from minority groups."[86]

Neither Ravitch nor Schlesinger was a detached observer. They co-authored a manifesto, "Statement of the Committee of Scholars in Defense of History," which was signed by twenty-six other academics and published in New York papers. The manifesto declared that the signees would "constitute [themselves] as a professional review committee to monitor and address the work of the Commissioner's panel."[87] Moreover, as a result of the conflict over a *Curriculum of Inclusion*, Schlesinger penned his response in *The Disuniting of America*, a book published by Whittle Communications, the firm that would later launch privatization efforts in public schools. Ravitch went further and distributed to members of a second committee revising the curriculum copies of a critical article on one of the Afrocentrists on the committee, Ali Mazrui.[88]

Ravitch and Schlesinger found support in the weekly columns of Albert Shanker in the *New York Times*. Shanker charged that the Task Force on Minorities report wanted "to make sure minority students get told nice stories about themselves," and they "want to make sure everybody gets equal time."[89] He pleaded that "we must strongly oppose any rewriting of history."[90]

Responding to the criticism, Commissioner Sobol authorized a second study by the task force, reconstituted with historians. Schlesinger became a consultant to the committee. The second report—*One Nation, Many Peoples: A Declaration of Cultural Interdependence*—was equivocal. On the one hand, the new report declared that "national unity does not require that we eliminate the very diversity that is the source of our uniqueness."[91] On the other hand, the report acknowledged that "special attention need be given to those values, characteristics, and traditions we have in common."[92]

The new social studies guidelines cited current scholarship. The report noted that "previous ideals of assimilation to an Anglo-American model have been put in question by recent scholarship in the universities."[93] Consequently, the authors of the guidelines argued that Americans "are no longer comfortable with the requirements, common in the past, that they shed their specific cultural differences in order to be considered American."[94]

One Nation, Many Peoples enunciated seven principles:

1. democracy—inculcating the idea of democratic government;
2. diversity—"understanding and respecting others and oneself";
3. economic and social justice—"understanding personal and social responsibility for economic and social systems";
4. globalism—comprehending world cultures;
5. ecological balance—understanding the changing natural environment;
6. ethics and values—"the pursuit of fairness and search for responsibility"; and
7. the individual and society—understanding the tensions between both.[95]

The curriculum guide provided examples of these principles. The report suggested a "need for multiple perspectives" to avoid a "We-They framework."[96] It also advised "language sensitivity" so that "the syllabi may not be deliberately or intentionally sexist, racist or prejudiced from the point of view of diversity."[97] Moreover, the examples used in a curriculum should not be limited since there has been, in the past, "a tendency to use white male examples of achievement."[98]

Some Western traditionalists on the committee dissented from the guide. Kenneth T. Jackson, a Columbia University historian, was in favor of a curriculum that recognized that "within any single country, one culture must be accepted as the standard."[99] Schlesinger also challenged the report in an addendum. He condemned "the ethnic interpretation" of the guide because it "reverses the historic theory of America—the creation of a new national culture and a *new* national identity."[100] Schlesinger charged that the report rejected "the very idea of assimilation."[101] Moreover, Schlesinger was uncomfortable with what he perceived to be a radical political impulse in the report: "I am also doubtful about the note occasionally sounded in the report that 'students must be taught social criticism' and 'see themselves as active makers and changers of culture and society' and 'promote economic fairness and social justice' and 'bring about change in their communities, the nation, and the world'. . . . I do not think it is the function of the schools to teach students to become reformers. . . . [L]et us not politicize the curriculum on behalf either of the left or right."[102] Once again the Western traditionalists had an ally in Albert Shanker. In his weekly column, Shanker denounced the second report as "dangerous."[103] What perplexed Shanker most was the concept of multiple perspectives in history. He interpreted that concept to mean that "the teaching of history should no longer be dominated by ideas that historians widely accepted."[104]

Afrocentrists on the committee were also not fully satisfied. Ellen Tedli was "supportive" but bemoaned the "little or no acknowledgement of the vast contribution of Africa, Asia, and the Americas to the development of Europe and the United States."[105] On the other hand, multiculturalists such as Catherine Cornbleth of the State University of New York–Buffalo considered *One Nation, Many Peoples* as "undermining the conventional 'heroes and contributions' approach to school history" while not constituting a "radical document."[106]

However, the attack of the Western traditionalists, which was widely reported in the media, resulted in the Board of Regents creating yet another committee to explore multiculturalism and curriculum.

CONCLUSION

Excellence reform in education signified the end of Henry Luce's "American Century." U.S. economic and military dominance was followed in this century with cultural and artistic influence in world affairs. As the economy of the United States declined and concomitantly the nation's worldwide influence, there was a national impetus to recharge American public education with a mission to restore American economic power. The schools thus became the battleground of a culture war, transported also to U.S. universities, that involved an agonizing reappraisal of American culture. The Western traditionalists who were excellence reformers, for the most part, invoked a glorified, romantic American past that may never have existed. In the end, this agonizing culture reappraisal was but one more indication of the decline of U.S. power in the world.

NOTES

1. James A. Banks, "The Culture Wars, Race and Education," *National Forum*, Fall 1993, p. 4.

2. National Commission on Excellence in Education, *A Nation at Risk: The Imperative for Educational Reform* (Washington, D.C.: U.S. Department of Education, April 1983), p. 24.

3. U.S. Department of Education, *America 2000: An Education Strategy* (Washington, D.C.: U.S. Government Printing Office, April 18, 1991), p. 9.

4. E. D. Hirsch, Jr., *Cultural Literacy: What Every American Needs to Know* (New York: Houghton Mifflin, 1987), p. 12.

5. *Ibid.*

6. *Ibid.*, pp. 1–2.

7. *Ibid.*, p. 5.

8. *Ibid.*, pp. xiv–xv.

9. *Ibid.*

10. *Ibid.*, p. xvii.

11. *Ibid.*, p. xiii.

12. *Ibid.*, pp. 94–98.

13. Benjamin Troutman, "A Caution on Cultural Literacy," *Currents* (Washington College), Summer 1988, p. 32.

14. *Ibid.*

15. *Virginian Ledger Star*, October 18, 1993, p. D3.

16. E. D. Hirsch, Jr., "Of Hooks, Tentacles, and Leaves," *Common Knowledge*, Summer 1993, p. 4.

17. *Core Knowledge* (promotional literature) (Charlottesville, Va.: Core Knowledge Foundation, Summer 1993), p. 6.

18. E. D. Hirsch, Jr. "Teach Knowledge, Not 'Mental Skills,' " *New York Times*, September 4, 1993, p. 19.

19. *Core Knowledge*, p. 6.

20. Albert Shanker, "Core Knowledge," *New York Times*, December 16, 1991, p. E7.

21. Herbert Kohl, "Rotten to the Core," *The Nation*, April 6, 1993, p. 458.

22. *Ibid.*

23. *Ibid.*

24. *Ibid.*, p. 460.

25. *Ibid.*

26. *Ibid.*, p. 461.

27. Hirsch, *Cultural Literacy*, p. viii.

28. Diane Ravitch, "Multiculturalism: E Pluribus Plures," in *Debating P.C.*, edited by Paul L. Berman (New York: Laurel, 1992), p. 278.

29. *Ibid.*, p. 273.

30. *Ibid.*, p. 280.

31. *Ibid.*, p. 275.

32. *Ibid.*, p. 295.
33. *Ibid.*, pp. 295–296.
34. *Ibid.*, p. 289.
35. *Ibid.*
36. Diane Ravitch and Abigail Thernstrom, eds. *The Democracy Reader* (New York: HarperCollins, 1992), p. xii.
37. *Ibid.*, p. 2.
38. *Ibid.*, p. 99.
39. *Ibid.*, p. xii.
40. Arthur M. Schlesinger, Jr., *The Disuniting of America: Reflections on a Multicultural Society* (New York: Whittle Books, 1991), p. 14.
41. *Ibid.*, p. 41.
42. Michael Katz, *Class, Bureaucracy, and Schools: The Illusion of Educational Change in America* (New York: Praeger, 1971), p. 39.
43. Schlesinger, *The Disuniting of America*, p. 53.
44. *Ibid.*
45. *Ibid.*
46. James W. Sanders, *The Education of an Urban Minority: Catholics in Chicago 1833–1965* (New York: Oxford University Press, 1977), p. 226.
47. Schlesinger, *The Disuniting of America*, p. 93.
48. *Ibid.*, pp. 75, 98.
49. *Ibid.*, p. 74.
50. *Ibid.*, p. 109.
51. *Ibid.*, p. 88.
52. *Ibid.*, p. 128.
53. William J. Bennett, *Our Children and Our Country: Improving America's Schools and Affirming the Common Culture* (New York: Simon and Schuster, 1988), p. 79.
54. Michael Bérubé, "Disuniting America Again," *The Journal of the Midwest Modern Language Association*, Spring 1993, pp. 35, 36, 38.
55. Catherine Cornbleth and Dexter Waugh, "The Greatest Speckled Bird: Education Policy-in-the-Making," *Educational Researcher*, October 1993, p. 31.
56. *Ibid.*, p. 32.
57. Molefi Kete Asante, *Afrocentricity* (Trenton, N.J.: Africa World Press, Inc., 1990), p. 1.
58. *Ibid.*, p. 6.
59. *Ibid.*, p. 27.
60. *Ibid.*, p. 89.
61. *Ibid.*, p. 6.
62. *Ibid.*, pp. 7–19.
63. *Ibid.*, p. 6.
64. *Ibid.*, p. 2.
65. Molefi Kete Asante, "Multiculturalism: An Exchange," in *Debating P.C.*, edited by Paul L. Berman (New York: Laurel, 1992), p. 308.
66. *Ibid.*
67. *Ibid.*, p. 311.
68. *Ibid.*
69. *Ibid.*, p. 307.

70. *Ibid.*, p. 309.

71. *Ibid.*, p. 301.

72. Joel Spring, *Wheels in the Head* (New York: McGraw-Hill, Inc., 1994), p. 108.

73. *Ibid.*

74. James A. Banks, "Multicultural Education: Development, Dimensions, and Challenges," *Phi Delta Kappan,* September 1993, p. 24.

75. *Ibid.*, p. 23.

76. *Ibid.*, p. 24.

77. *Ibid.*, p. 23.

78. *Ibid.*, p. 24.

79. Banks, "The Culture Wars," p. 40.

80. Banks, "Multicultural Education," p. 24.

81. New York State Task Force on Minorities, *A Curriculum of Inclusion* (Albany: New York State Department of Education, July 1989), p. iii.

82. *Ibid.*, p. iv.

83. Diane Ravitch, "Multiculturalism," pp. 291–292.

84. *Ibid.*

85. Schlesinger, *The Disuniting of America,* p. 66.

86. *Ibid.*, p. 68.

87. Cornbleth and Waugh, "The Great Speckled Bird," p. 34.

88. *Ibid.*, p. 35.

89. Albert Shanker, "The Sobol Report," *New York Times,* January 28, 1990, p. E7.

90. *Ibid.*

91. Thomas Sobol, New York State Commissioner of Education, "Understanding Diversity," memorandum to New York State Board of Regents, July 12, 1991, p. 7.

92. *Ibid.*

93. New York State Social Studies Review and Development Committee, *One Nation, Many Peoples: A Declaration of Cultural Interdependence* (Albany: New York State Department of Education, June 1991), p. xi.

94. *Ibid.*

95. *Ibid.*, pp. 8–11.

96. *Ibid.*, p. 18.

97. *Ibid.*, p. 19.

98. *Ibid.*, p. 20.

99. *Ibid.*, p. 39.

100. *Ibid.*, p. 45.

101. *Ibid.*, p. 46.

102. *Ibid.*, p. 47.

103. Albert Shanker, "Multiple Perspectives," *New York Times,* October 27, 1991, p. E7.

104. *Ibid.*

105. New York State Social Studies Review and Development Committee, *One Nation, Many Peoples,* p. 48.

106. Cornbleth and Waugh, "The Great Speckled Bird," p. 35.

CHAPTER EIGHT

CONCLUSION

There are a number of observations to be made about the similarities of the three great educational reform movements. First, these reform movements were the result of outside societal pressures. No major educational reform movement in the United States was caused by intrinsic educational forces. This phenomenon prompts speculation that deep-seated educational reform cannot occur without larger movements within society. Second, the progressive reform movement set the stage for the educational reform movements that followed. The equity reform movement was compatible with progressive reform and sought to fulfill the unfinished progressive agenda of educating the poor. On the other hand, the excellence reform movement constituted a repudiation of both progressive and equity reform. Excellence reform discarded the progressive concept of development for content-based curricula. It also shifted the reform focus from educating the poor to educating the best and brightest. Third, both the progressive and equity reformers shared a romantic concept of the poor. Fourth, progressive reform and equity reform were dominated by political liberals and radicals. On the other hand, excellence reform was championed, for the most part, by political conservatives. Fifth, U.S. presidents became more involved in establishing a national educational agenda. After World War II the nation became a global economic power relying on technology. The emergence of a sophisticated economy required higher levels of education. Consequently, education became a national priority. Sixth, all three reform movements gave rise to a new breed of reformer: the scholar/activist. John Dewey provided a role model of the scholar as activist. The scholar/activist reemerged in the equity and excellence reform movements. A seventh common denominator was an emphasis on innovation. At its best, this focus on innovation spawned a plethora of new ideas. At its worst, the emphasis on the new often brought with it faddism. New programs were often hastily implemented and allowed to disappear after a short period of time. For example, philanthropist Walter Annenberg's gift of a half billion dollars to the federal government's New American Schools Development Corporation in 1993 sought to promote innovation.[1] Equally important, educational reformers pursued comprehensive change. Moreover, this comprehensive change was often accompanied by the messianic zeal of the respective reformers. Eight, educational change became more based on scholarship. By the 1960s, educational research, following the example of social science research, became more sophisticated. Experimental designs with inferential statistics were applied to classroom settings. Moreover, qualitative research, borrowing from anthropologist methodologies such as participant-observation, were now used. In short, educational policy became research based.

more research based

Finally, perhaps the greatest weakness in educational reform, as the century neared its end, was the lack of a clear educational vision transcending the societal pressures that created major educational reform. Whereas John Dewey provided that vision for nearly half a century, no successor for the new century was on the horizon. Instead, educational reform has become fragmented. We now have thinkers who specialize. We will examine a few of these thinkers: Amy Gutman on democracy and education; Allan Bloom on the great ideas of Western civilization; Henry Giroux on the resistance of dominated groups; and Lawrence Kohlberg on moral education.

AMY GUTMAN AND POLITICAL EDUCATION

Amy Gutman presented the first major interpretation of democratic education since Dewey. In her 1987 treatise *Democratic Education*, Gutman, a professor of political philosophy at Princeton, perceived education to be essential to the preservation of democracy.

For Gutman, the *raison d'être of* education was to insure that citizens are sufficiently educated to preserve democracy. First, Gutman assumed political democracy to be the ideal. Second, she viewed the role of education as "the stage for democratic politics" and as playing "a central role in it."[2] For democracy to succeed, she argued, "democratic politics puts a high premium on citizens being both knowledgeable and articulate."[3] She was emphatic on that point. Her central vision was that "we can conclude that 'political education'—the cultivation of the virtues, knowledge, and skills necessary for political participation—has moral primacy over the other purposes of public education in a democratic society."[4] In short, education exists to serve the democratic state. On the other hand, Dewey's formulation equated the two as serving each other: education for democracy, and democracy for education. Dewey perceived the fulfillment of the whole individual as having primacy over other objectives.

Gutman wrestled over the question of majoritarian rule. In order to keep majoritarian rule in check, she proposed a theory of nonrepression and nondiscrimination. That is, democracy should be prevented from discriminating and repressing minority interests. Her theory of nonrepression and nondiscrimination is indebted to Harvard philosopher John Rawls's definition of justice in his classic 1971 work *A Theory of Justice*. Rawls argued that the just society must attempt to be fair. He defined fairness as achieving an equilibrium where all parties involved have a degree of satisfaction.

Gutman applied her theory of nonrepression and nondiscrimination to the controversial issue of affirmative action. She discounted racial quotas but not "all ways of discriminating *in favor* of blacks."[5] Gutman also extended affirmative action so that it "applies equally well to the case of other disadvantaged minorities and women."[6]

Gutman took a centrist position that assumed that democracy proceeds from *rationality*—a word common in her text. However, she did not sufficiently emphasize the confrontational politics that dominated groups must often pursue. Her arguments presumed "that reasonable" men and women will negotiate social justice. A closer reading of U.S. history reveals class, racial, and feminist strife with incremental gains at best.

ALLAN BLOOM AND THE GREAT IDEAS OF WESTERN MAN

Although Allan Bloom's 1987 book *The Closing of the American Mind*, specifically deals with the American university, this national best seller set the stage for conservative influence that sought to redirect American education. Bloom, then a professor of philosophy at the University of Chicago, advocated a return to a core curriculum based on the Great Books of Western civilization. He argued that "the only serious solution" to the alleged decline of the American university and American education was "that almost universally rejected . . . gold old Great Books approach."[7] Bloom simply recycled Robert Maynard Hutchins's proposal of the 1930s.

Moreover, according to Bloom, these Great Books should be grounded mainly in Western thought. In his experience, college students were "natural savages" who had "hardly heard the names of the writers . . . across the Atlantic."[8] Bloom was not enamored of American culture. For Bloom, "America's greatest thoughts were in our political system."[9] There was "never a native plant";[10] America was ever "dependent on Europe," and all of "our peaks were derivative."[11] Moreover, Bloom advocated an elitist system of education. He believed that education was really the province of "the thousands of students of comparative high intelligence" who attend "the twenty or thirty best universities" and who "are the most likely to have the greatest moral and intellectual effect on the nation."[12] In short, Bloom updated the concept of democratic education based on meritocracy.

The Closing of the American Mind consisted of a repudiation of the 1960s and the surge toward social justice. Bloom stated the case for political and educational conservatives: "By the mid-sixties, universities were offering [students] every concession other than education, but appeasement failed and soon the whole experiment in excellence was washed away, leaving not a trace."[13]

Bloom summed up the 1960s as an era out of which "nothing positive" came.[14] He contended that during the 1960s "not a single book of lasting importance was produced."[15] Consequently he was alarmed at the demand for more equality from minorities and women. He characterized the Black Power movement as erroneously based on a misinterpretation that the Constitution was a "defense of slavery."[16] He maintained that "affirmative action now institutionalizes the worst aspect of separation."[17]

Philosophically, Bloom condemned the moral relativism he believed to be prevalent in American society and education. He traced that moral relativism to Dewey. Bloom scorned "liberalism without natural rights," which he perceived as "the kind we knew from . . . John Dewey" and which, he alleged, ignored "fundamental values."[18]

Bloom's book enjoyed immense popularity. It dovetailed with the work of E. D. Hirch, Jr., Diane Ravitch, and Arthur Schlesinger, Jr.

HENRY GIROUX AND THE THEORY OF RESISTANCE

At the other end of the ideological spectrum is Henry Giroux and his theory of resistance. A professor of education at Miami University of Ohio, Giroux authored numerous books advocating school reform in order to empower disenfranchised minorities. Giroux's vision of a democratic culture blended the theories of the Brazilian educator Paulo Freire and the neo-Marxist Herbert Marcuse.

In order to fully comprehend Giroux, one must confront the work of Freire, whose radical ideas of teaching literacy prompted the totalitarian Brazilian government to expel him in the 1970s. He remained in exile for nearly a generation until a more democratic government permitted him to return. Freire's experience in a totalitarian right-wing nation led him to believe that teaching poor peasants to read required a revolutionary methodology. He devised a method whereby the best way for a poor person to learn was by first understanding his or her victimization.

Freire's classic work was *Pedagogy of the Oppressed*, published in 1971 in the United States. As one of that book's first reviewers, I found Freire to have published a seminal text. I described Freire's methodology as follows: "Freire's main insight is that victims must develop a political awareness of their condition before they can sufficiently master the resources to develop their learning potentials. Once the victim truly perceives the cause of his affliction and the revolutionary course to change that condition, he is free to learn."[19] In my assessment of Freire, I concluded that he had pushed "the relationship between politics and education to its extreme" and termed his method "educopolitics."[20] I felt that "Freire is beyond us at that moment, ahead of his time" because oppression "was far more total in Latin America that in the United States."[21] Still, I speculated that "Freire's insights and command of political realities may, in time, prove to be correct for us in the United States."[22]

Freire developed a following in the United States with black and Hispanic school activists and leftist reformers. Twenty years after the publication of *Pedagogy of the Oppressed*, his book was chosen by a panel of "educators, public school activists, scholars and writers" for "the activists library" as being one of the most influential.[23] A Hispanic professor characterized *Pedagogy of the Oppressed* as helping "us to fashion an education that . . . challenges us to see life, and possibility."[24] (Another Hispanic professor chose one of Grioux's books because it "provides us with powerful arguments against neoconservative attempts" to reform public education.[25])

Giroux's key work was *Theory and Resistance in Education: A Pedagogy for the Opposition*. With an introduction by Freire, the book sought to make education "emancipatory."[26] Giroux perceived a "politics of the hidden curriculum" that girds public schooling.[27] Public schools are more than "instructional sites," he argued; they are "cultural and political sites" that "represent areas of contestation and struggle among differently empowered cultural and economic groups."[28] Giroux believed that public schools are tilted against the poor due to "the dialectical interplay of social interest, political power and economic power" of the majority that results in the fashioning of "school knowledge and practice."[29] Consequently, Giroux contended that "schools produce social formations around class, gender, and racial exploitation."[30]

According to Giroux, what is lacking is an emancipatory educational theory. He stated his case: "educational theory and practice stands at an impasse. . . . [It] remains caught in a theoretical legacy that has plagued social theory in general, and Marxism in particular, for decades."[31] He proclaimed an educational theory that would radically restructure American society. Again, Giroux is clear on this purpose: "If citizenship education is to be *emancipatory* it must begin with the assumption that its major aim is not to fit students into the existing society; instead, its primary purpose must be to stimulate their passions, imaginations, and intellects so that they will be moved to *challenge* the social, political, and economic forces that weigh so heavily upon their lives" (emphasis added).[32]

Nevertheless, Giroux's prescriptions are an amalgam of Dewey, Freire, and Lawrence Kohlberg. He proposed five steps to revolutionize education. First, schools should stimulate "the active nature of students' " participation; second, students must be taught "to think critically"; third, they must "develop a critical mode of reasoning"; fourth, they must be taught "to clarify values"; and fifth, students must "learn about the structural and ideological forces that influence and restrict their lives."[33]

Giroux advanced the cause of dominated groups. Unfortunately, his analysis suffered from Marxist dogmatism. He weighed class more heavily in his triad of class, gender, and race. Giroux repeated the error of the old-line American socialists of the 1960s who dismissed both the Black Power phase of the Civil Rights Movement and the anti-war protest movement. Of the community control movement, Giroux concluded that the "community control advocates made no profound critique of the existing curriculum."[34] By the 1990s, he would dismiss much of the multicultural movement in education as "identity politics":

Identity politics since the 1960's has played a significant role in refiguring a variety of human experiences within a discourse in which diverse political views, sexual orientations, races, ethnicities, and cultural differences are taken up ... [but] it often failed to move beyond a notion of difference ... [so that oppressed groups] often substituted one master narrative for another, invoked a politics of separatism, ... [and were guilty of] moralism, antiintellectualism and suspect romanticization of authentic experiences.[35]

In short, these revolutionary movements did not conform to Giroux's preexisting Marxist grid.

LAWRENCE KOHLBERG AND MORAL DEVELOPMENT

Perhaps the most influential educator since Dewey has been Lawrence Kohlberg with his theory of moral development. A Harvard professor of psychology and philosophy, Kohlberg conducted research over a fifteen-year period into the early 1970s on the development of a moral sense with a group of seventy-five boys. He concluded that moral development occurred within "a sequence of moral stages."[36]

Kohlberg posited six such stages. First, a youth in the early years comprehends little difference between moral and social or physical values. Second, a youth discovers values that are intrinsic to his or her needs. Third, a youth perceives values relating to family and other associates. Fourth, a person grounds values in religious rights and duties. Fifth, a youth understands values as part of a larger community. Last, a person understands values as a universal moral principle. Most important, Kohlberg held that moral development can be molded by schooling, and he ventured a number of educational experiments.

Kohlberg was influenced primarily by the psychologist Jean Piaget and by John Dewey. Of his debt to Piaget, Kohlberg declared that "following Piaget" and his "theory of development," he could find "the same is true in the area of moral development."[37] And with Dewey he perceived "development as the aim of education."[38] He summed up his reverence for both: "the development-philosophical strategy for defining educational objectives, which emerges from the work of Dewey and Piaget, is a theoretical rationale that withstands logical criticism and is consistent with, if not 'proved' by, current research findings."[39] Kohlberg was also influenced by his Harvard colleague John Rawls. Rawls advanced three stages of moral development, and Kohlberg noted "the similarities in assumption between Rawls' theory and my own."[40]

At Harvard, Kohlberg taught a graduate seminar entitled Moral Development and Moral Education. His reading list had but four books: Plato's *Republic*, Emile Durkheim's *Moral Education*; Jean Piaget's *Moral Judgment of the Child*; and John Dewey's *Democracy and Education.*[41]

Kohlberg observed in his research that each individual proceeds toward various stages of development. He concluded that "there were universal ontogenetic trends toward the development of morality as it has been conceived by Western moral philosophers."[42] The trick, then, is to instill higher levels of moral development in youth through schooling. Kohlberg criticized "the fallacy of value neutrality," that is, that schools did not deal with value.[43] He argued that schools imparted some values as part of a hidden curriculum. Kohlberg sought to guide moral development through schooling. Thus, Kohlberg became the father of the "values clarification" movement.

Unfortunately, Kohlberg, in his research on schooling, was able to show that students moved only to a third stage, namely a moral sense relating to association with family and peer groups. Schools have been unable to develop the highest stage of morality whereby a youth guides his or her action on the basis of a universal moral principle.[44]

Kohlberg's research was questioned by a former student and collaborator, feminist scholar Carol Gilligan. She criticized Kohlberg for his selection of males and exclusion of females in his study. In her research on moral development with females, she found another perspective. She argued that the very values most cherished among girls were precisely those that had lesser importance in Kohlberg's schemata. In her 1982 book, *In a Different Voice: Psychological Theory and Women's Development,* Gilligan noted that:

Prominent among those who thus appear to be deficient in moral development when measured by Kohlberg's scale are women, whose judgments seem to exemplify the third stage of his six-stage sequence. . . .

Yet herein lies a paradox, for the very traits that traditionally have defined "goodness" of women, their care for and sensitivity to the needs of others, are those that mark them as deficient in moral development.[45]

Thus, Gilligan revised her mentor's work. Nevertheless, Kohlberg advanced the inquiry on moral character and how schools may influence students' values.

SUMMARY

As the close of the twentieth century approaches, some fundamental questions concerning public education and American society have yet to be resolved. The purpose of schooling remains unclear. The equity reform movement was most interested in providing social and economic mobility for the poor. Excellence reform strove to restore America's economic might. Only the progressive movement sought to answer the question of what is the ultimate purpose of education: that is, to develop the whole person's abilities—intellectual, social, artistic, and moral.

However, the aim of education depends on the nature and purpose of society. There still exists a division in the American mind over what kind of society we desire. Some propose a narrow society based on political democracy with a meritocratic educational system. Others seek a social democracy incorporating an egalitarian educational system. Until the larger question of what type of American society we want is answered, educational reform may continue to be subject to the whims of the larger society.

NOTES

1. *New York Times*, December 18, 1993, p. 9.

2. Amy Gutman, *Democratic Education* (Princeton, N.J.: Princeton University Press, 1987), p. 3.

3. *Ibid.*, p. 285.

4. *Ibid.*, p. 287.

5. *Ibid.*, p. 204.

6. *Ibid.*

7. Allan Bloom, *The Closing of the American Mind* (New York: Simon and Schuster, 1987), p. 344.

8. *Ibid.*, p. 48.
9. *Ibid.*, p. 321.
10. *Ibid.*
11. *Ibid.*
12. *Ibid.*, p. 27.
13. *Ibid.*, p. 50.
14. *Ibid.*, p. 320.
15. *Ibid.*, p. 321.
16. *Ibid.*, p. 33.
17. *Ibid.*, p. 96.
18. *Ibid.*, p. 29.
19. Maurice R. Berube, "Educopolitics," *Social Policy*, November/December 1971, p. 60.
20. *Ibid.*
21. *Ibid.*, p. 61.
22. *Ibid.*
23. "The School Activists' Library," *The Nation*, September 21, 1992, p. 296.
24. *Ibid.*, p. 299.
25. *Ibid.*, p. 295.
26. Henry A. Giroux, *Theory and Resistance in Education: A Pedagogy for the Opposition* (South Hadley, Mass.: Bergin and Garvey, 1983), p. 32.
27. *Ibid.*, p. 20.
28. *Ibid.*, p. 32.
29. *Ibid.*, p. 47.
30. *Ibid.*, p. 30.
31. *Ibid.*, p. 31.
32. *Ibid.*, p. 201.
33. *Ibid.*, pp. 202–203.
34. Stanley Aronowitz and Henry A. Giroux, *Education Under Siege: A Conservative, Liberal and Radical Debate Over Schooling* (South Hadley, Mass.: Bergin and Garvey, 1985), p. 3.
35. Henry A. Giroux, *Living Dangerously: Multiculturalism and the Politics of Difference* (New York: Peter Lang, 1993), pp. 92–93.
36. Lawrence Kohlberg, *The Philosophy of Moral Development*, vol. 1 (New York: Harper & Row, 1981), p. 133.
37. *Ibid.*
38. *Ibid.*, p. 86.
39. *Ibid.*, p. 49.
40. *Ibid.*, p. 193.
41. *Ibid.*, p. ix.
42. *Ibid.*, p. 10.
43. *Ibid.*, p. 64.
44. Gutman, *Democratic Education*, p. 60.
45. Carol Gilligan, *In a Different Voice: Psychological Theory and Women's Development* (Cambridge, Mass.: Harvard University Press, 1982), p. 18.

BIBLIOGRAPHY

BOOKS

Addams, Jane. *Twenty Years at Hull House.* New York: Macmillan Co., 1945.
————. *Democracy and Social Ethics.* Cambridge, Mass.: Harvard University Press, 1964.
Adelson, Alan. *SDS.* New York: Charles Scribner's Sons, 1972.
Allen, Gay Wilson. *William James: A Biography.* New York: Viking Press, 1967.
Ambrose, Stephen E. *Eisenhower: The President,* vol. 2, New York: Simon and Schuster, 1983.
Ariés, Phillipe. *Centuries of Childhood.* New York: Vintage Books, 1962.
Aronowitz, Stanley, and Henry A. Giroux. *Education Under Siege: A Conservative, Liberal and Radical Debate Over Schooling.* South Hadley, Mass.: Bergin and Garvey, 1985.
Asante, Molefi Kete. *Afrocentricity.* Trenton, N.J.: Africa World Press, Inc., 1990.
Banfield, Edward. *The Unheavenly City.* Boston: Little, Brown, 1970.
Bennett, William J. *Our Children and Our Country: Improving America's Schools and Affirming the Common Culture.* New York: Simon and Schuster, 1988.
Berman, Paul L., ed. *Debating P.C.* New York: Laurel, 1992.
Berrueta-Clement, John R., et al. *Changed Lives: The Effects of the Perry Preschool Program on Youths Through Age 19.* Ypsilanti, Mich.: High/Scope Press, 1984.
Berube, Maurice R. *Teacher Politics: The Influence of Unions.* Westport, Conn.: Greenwood Press, 1988.
Berube, Maurice R., and Marilyn Gittell, eds. *Confrontation at Ocean Hill–Brownsville.* New York: Praeger, 1969.
Bloom, Allan. *The Closing of the American Mind.* New York: Simon and Schuster, 1987.

Body-Gendrot, Sophie. *Ville et Violence*. Paris: Presses Universitaires de France, 1993.

Cashman, Sean Dennis. *American in the Age of the Titans: The Progressive Era and World War I*. New York: New York University Press, 1988.

Chubb, John E., and Terry M. Moe. *Politics, Markets and American Schools*. Washington, D.C.: Brookings Institution, 1990.

Coleman, James, et al. *Equality of Educational Opportunity*. Washington, D.C.: U.S. Government Printing Office, 1966.

Counts, George S. *Dare the School Build a New Social Order?* New York: Arno Press, 1969.

Cremin, Lawrence A. *The Transformation of the School: Progressivism in American Education 1876–1957*. New York: Vintage, 1961.

Dewey, John. *The School and Society*. Chicago: University of Chicago Press, 1900.

———. *Democracy and Education*. New York: The Macmillan Co., 1931.

Dewey, John, and Evelyn Dewey. *Schools of To-Morrow*. New York: E. P. Dutton, 1915.

DuBois, W.E.B. *The Autobiography of W.E.B. DuBois*. New York: International Publishers, 1968.

———. *The Education of Black People: Ten Critiques 1906–1960*. Amherst: University of Massachusetts Press, 1973.

Dykhuizen, George. *The Life and Mind of John Dewey*. Carbondale: Southern Illinois University Press, 1973.

Ekirch, Arthur A., Jr. *Progressivism in America*. New York: New Viewpoints, 1974.

Freire, Paulo. *Pedagogy of the Oppressed*. New York: Seabury Press, 1970.

Friedman, Benjamin M. *Day of Reckoning: The Consequences of American Economic Policy Under Reagan and After*. New York: Random House, 1988.

Garrow, David J. *Bearing the Cross: Martin Luther King, Jr., and the Southern Christian Leadership Conference*. New York: William Morrow and Co., 1986.

Gettleman, Marvin, and David Mermelstein, eds. *The Great Society Reader*. New York: Random House, 1967.

Gilligan, Carol. *In a Different Voice: Psychological Theory and Women's Development*. Cambridge, Mass.: Harvard University Press, 1982.

Giroux, Henry A. *Theory and Resistance in Education: A Pedagogy for the Opposition*. South Hadley, Mass.: Bergin and Garvey, 1983.

———. *Living Dangerously: Multiculturalism and the Politics of Difference*. New York: Peter Lang, 1993.

Gittell, Marilyn, with Maurice R. Berube et al. *Local Control in Education: Three Demonstration School Districts in New York City*. New York: Praeger, 1972.

———. *School Boards and School Policy: An Evaluation of Decentralization in New York City*. New York: Praeger, 1973.

Glazer, Nathan. *Affirmative Discrimination*. New York: Basic Books, 1975.

Grant, Gerald D., ed. *Review of Research in Education 18*. Washington, D.C.: American Educational Research Association, 1992.

Greer, Colin. *The Great School Legend*. New York: Basic Books, 1972.

Gross, Beatrice, and Ronald Gross, eds. *The Great School Debates*. New York: Simon and Schuster, 1985.

Gould, Lewis L., ed. *The Progressive Era*. Syracuse, N.Y.: Syracuse University Press, 1979.

Gutman, Amy. *Democratic Education.* Princeton, N.J.: Princeton University Press, 1987.

Haley, Alex. *The Autobiography of Malcolm X.* New York: Ballantine Books Edition, February, 1992.

Hampton, Henry, and Steve Fayer. *Voices of Freedom: An Oral History of the Civil Rights Movement from the 1950s through the 1980s.* New York: Bantam Books, 1990.

Harrington, Michael. *The Other America: Poverty in the United States.* New York: The Macmillan Co., 1962.

———. *The New American Poverty.* New York: Holt, Rinehart and Winston, 1984.

———. *The Long Distance Runner: An Autobiography.* New York: Holt, 1988.

Hirsch, E. D., Jr. *Cultural Literacy: What Every American Needs to Know.* New York: Houghton Mifflin, 1987.

Hofstader, Richard. *The Age of Reform.* New York: Alfred A. Knopf, 1955.

James, William. *Talks to Teachers.* New York: Henry Holt and Co., 1925.

Jencks, Christopher, et al. *Inequality.* New York: Basic Books, 1973.

Katz, Michael. *Class, Bureaucracy and the Schools: The Illusion of Educational Change in America.* New York: Praeger, 1971.

Kaufman, Jonathan. *Broken Alliance: The Turbulent Times Between Blacks and Jews in America.* New York: Charles Scribner's Sons, 1988.

King, Martin Luther, Jr. *Where Do We Go From Here?* New York: Harper & Row, 1967.

Kluger, Richard. *Simple Justice: The History of Brown v. Board of Education and Black America's Struggle for Equality.* New York: Alfred A. Knopf, 1976.

Kohlberg, Lawrence. *The Philosophy of Moral Development,* vol. 1. New York: Harper & Row, 1981.

Kozol, Jonathan. *Death at an Early Age: The Destruction of the Hearts and Minds of Negro Children in the Boston Public Schools.* Boston: Houghton Mifflin, 1967.

———. *Savage Inequalities.* New York: Crown Publishers, 1991.

Levine, Naomi, with Richard Cohen. *Ocean Hill–Brownsville: A Case History of Schools in Crisis.* New York: Popular Library, 1969.

Lissak, Rivka Shpak. *Pluralism and Progressives: Hull House and the New Immigrant 1890–1919.* Chicago: University of Chicago Press, 1989.

Marable, Manning. *Race, Reform and Rebellion: The Second Reconstruction in Black America, 1945–1990.* Jackson: University Press of Mississippi, 1991.

Mayer, Martin. *The Teachers Strike.* New York: Harper & Row, 1968.

McCluskey, Neil G. *Public Schools and Moral Education.* New York: Columbia University Press, 1958.

McDannell, Colleen, and Bernhard Lang. *Heaven: A History.* New Haven, Conn.: Yale University Press, 1988.

Miller, Herbert Adolphus. *The School and the Immigrant.* Philadelphia: Wm. F. Fell Co., 1916.

Moynihan, Daniel P. *Maximum Feasible Misunderstanding.* New York: Free Press, 1969.

Peters, R. S., ed. *John Dewey Reconsidered.* London: Routledge and Kegan Paul, 1977.

Postman, Neil, and Charles Weingartner. *The School Book.* New York: Delacorte Press, 1973.

Rauschenbusch, Walter. *Christianity and the Social Crisis.* New York: The Macmillan Co., 1924.

Ravitch, Diane. *The Great School Wars.* New York: Basic Books, 1974.

———. *The Troubled Crusade: American Education 1945–1980.* New York: Basic Books, 1983.

Ravitch, Diane, and Abigail Thernstrom, eds. *The Democracy Reader.* New York: HarperCollins, 1992.

Rice, Joseph Mayer. *The Public-School System of the United States.* New York: Arno Press, 1969.

Rickover, Hyman G. *Education and Freedom.* New York: E. P. Dutton, 1959.

Riis, Jacob. *How the Other Half Lives.* New York: Charles Scribner's Sons, 1920.

Rousseau, Jean Jacques. *Emilé: or an Education.* New York: Basic Books, 1979.

Rugg, Harold, and Ann Schumaker. *The Child-Centered School.* Yonkers, N.Y.: World Book Co., 1928.

Sanders, James. W. *The Education of an Urban Minority: Catholics in Chicago 1833–1965.* New York: Oxford University Press, 1977.

Schlesinger, Arthur M., Jr. *The Disuniting of America: Reflections on a Multicultural Society.* New York: Whittle Books, 1991.

Selden, David. *The Teacher Rebellion.* Washington, D.C.: Howard University Press, 1985.

Shannon, David. A. *The Socialist Party of America.* Chicago: Quadrangle Books, 1955.

Sleeper, Jim. *The Closest of Strangers: Liberalism and the Politics of Race in New York.* New York: W. W. Norton, 1990.

Spring, Joel. *Education and the Corporate State.* Boston: Beacon Press, 1972.

———. *Conflict of Interests: The Politics of American Education.* White Plains, N.Y.: Longman, 1993.

———. *Wheels in the Head.* New York: McGraw-Hill, Inc., 1994.

Thurow, Lester C. *The Zero-Sum Society.* New York: Penguin Books, 1981.

———. *Head to Head: The Coming Economic Battle Among Japan, Europe and America.* New York: William Morrow and Co., 1992.

Toffler, Alvin, ed. *The Schoolhouse in the City.* New York: Praeger, 1968.

Ture, Kwame (Stokely Carmichael), and Charles V. Hamilton. *Black Power: The Politics of Liberation.* New York: Vintage Edition, 1992.

Urofsky, Melvin, ed. *Why Teachers Strike: Teacher Rights and Community Control.* New York: Anchor Books, 1970.

U.S. Civil Rights Commission. *Racial Isolation in the Public Schools.* Washington, D.C.: U.S. Government Printing Office, 1967.

Van De Burg, William L. *New Day in Babylon: The Black Power Movement in America.* Chicago: University of Chicago Press, 1992.

Weinberg, Meyer. *The Search for Quality Integrated Education.* Westport, Conn.: Greenwood Press, 1983.

Willie, Charles V., Antoine M. Earibalds, and Wornie L. Reed. *The Education of African-Americans.* New York: Auburn House, 1991.

Wilson, William Julius. *The Truly Disadvantaged.* Chicago: University of Chicago Press, 1987.

X, Malcolm. *February 1965: The Final Speeches.* New York: Pathfinder Press, 1992.

REPORTS AND UNPUBLISHED MATERIALS

Barner, George. *The Ocean Hill–Brownsville Community Views the News Coverage.* New York: Center for New York City Affairs, December 1968.

Beales, Janet R., and John O'Leary. *Making Schools Work: Contracting Options for Better Management.* Los Angeles: Reason Foundation, November 1993.

Carpenter, Joseph, Jr. *The Leadership Philosophy of Dr. Martin Luther King, Jr.: Its Educational Implications.* Ph.D. dissertation. Ann Arbor: University of Michigan, 1971.

Halperin, Samuel, ed. *Voices from the Field: 30 Expert Opinions on America 2000, the Bush Administration Strategy to "Reinvent" America's Schools.* Washington, D.C.: William T. Grant Foundation Commission on Work, Family and Citizenship, Institute for Educational Leadership, 1991.

Holley, Ann-Carol Banton. *A Comparative Study of the Effects of Two Urban Kindergarten Beginning Reading Programs on Student Oral Reading Performance and Attitudes Toward Reading.* Ph.D. dissertation. Norfolk, Va.: Old Dominion University, 1988.

Howe, Harold, II. "Oral History Interview." Transcript. Austin, Tex.: Lyndon Baines Johnson Presidential Library, July 12, 1968.

Lazar, Irving, and Richard B. Darlington. *Lasting Effects After Preschool.* Ithaca, N.Y.: Cornell University, October 1978.

Moore, Donald R., and Suzanne Davenport. *School Choice: The New and Improved Sorting Machine.* Chicago: Designs for Change, February 1989.

National Alliance for Business. *The Compact Project: Final Report.* Washington, D.C.: National Alliance for Business, 1991.

National Commission on Excellence in Education. *A Nation at Risk: The Imperative for Educational Reform.* Washington, D.C.: U.S. Department of Education, 1983.

New York State Social Studies Review and Development Committee. *One Nation, Many Peoples: A Declaration of Cultural Interdependence.* Albany: New York State Department of Education, June 1991.

New York State Task Force on Minorities. *A Curriculum of Inclusion.* Albany: New York State Department of Education, July 1989.

Orfield, Gary, and Franklin Monfort et al. *Status of School Desegregation: The Next Generation.* Cambridge, Mass.: Harvard University Metropolitan Opportunity Project, January 8, 1992.

U.S. Department of Commerce. *Population Profile of the United States 1993.* Washington, D.C.: Government Printing Office, 1993.

U.S. Department of Education. *America 2000: An Education Strategy.* Washington, D.C.: U.S. Government Printing Office, April 18, 1991.

———. *Goals 2000: Educate America Act.* Washington, D.C.: U.S. Government Printing Office, October 1993.

ARTICLES

Armor, David. J. "The Evidence on Busing." *The Public Interest*, Summer 1972.

Aronowitz, Stanley. "A Reply to Maurice R. Berube's 'Social Change and the White Working Class.' " *Social Policy*, September/October 1970.

Aronowitz, Stanley, and Henry A. Giroux. "Hope for Our Schools: A New Manifesto for Education." *Village Voice*, October 4, 1988.

Association for Supervision and Curriculum. "Guidelines for Business Involvement in the Schools." *Educational Leadership*, December 1989/January 1990.

Banks, James A. "The Culture Wars, Race and Education." *National Forum*, Fall 1993.

———. "Multicultural Education: Development, Dimensions, and Challenges." *Phi Delta Kappan*, September 1993.

Barrow, Clyde W. "Charles A. Beard's Social Democracy: A Critique of the Populist-Progressive Style in American Political Thought." *Polity*, Winter 1988.

Berube, Maurice R. "Black Power Comes to School." *The United Teacher* (United Federation of Teachers AFL-CIO), September 22, 1966.

———. "Educopolitics." *Social Policy*, November/December 1971.

Bérubé, Michael. "Disuniting America Again." *The Journal of the Midwest Modern Language Association*, Spring 1993.

"The Boston Compact Fosters City-wide Collaboration." *Educational Record*, Fall 1987/Winter 1988.

Brachel, Jessica Skelly von. "How Business Helps the Schools." *Fortune*, October 21, 1991.

Carr, Leslie G., and Donald J. Ziegler. "White Flight and White Return in Norfolk: A Test of Predictions." *Sociology of Education*, vol. 63, 1990.

Clark, Donald M. "School Business Partnerships Are Too Much Talk and Not Enough Performance." *The American School Board Journal*, August 1988.

Cornbleth, Catherine, and Dexter Waugh. "The Great Speckled Bird: Education Policy-in-the-Making." *Educational Researcher*. October 1993.

Cuban, Larry. "The Corporate Myth of Reforming Public Schools." *Phi Delta Kappan*, October 1992.

Dewey, John. "Professional Organization of Teachers." *American Teacher* (American Federation of Teachers, AFL), September 1916.

———. "How Much Freedom in New Schools?" *The New Republic*, July 9, 1930.

DuBois, W.E.B. "Does the Negro Need Separate Schools?" *Journal of Negro Education*, July 1935.

Eisenhower, Dwight D. "The Private Letters of the President." *Life*, March 16, 1959.

Filene, Peter G. "An Obituary for the 'Progressive Movement.' " *American Quarterly*, Spring 1970.

Flygare, Thomas J. "A Return to Neighborhood Schools as a Way of Stemming 'White Flight.' " *Phi Delta Kappan*, May 1986.

Foner, Eric. "The Education of Richard Hofstader." *The Nation*, May 4, 1992.

Fordham, Signithia, and John U. Ogbu. "Black Students' School Success: Coping with the Burden of 'Acting White.' " *The Urban Review*, vol. 18, no. 3, 1986.

Greeley, Andrew. "The Ethnic Miracle." *The Public Interest*, Fall 1976.

Hirsch, E. D., Jr. "Of Hooks, Tentacles, and Leaves." *Common Knowledge* (Core Knowledge Foundation), Summer 1983.

———. "Teach Knowledge, Not 'Mental Skills.' " *New York Times*, September 4, 1993.

Ichimura, Takahisa. "The Protestant Assumption in Progressive Educational Thought." *Teachers College Record*, Spring 1984.

Ikpa, Vivian. "Gender, Race, Chapter I Participation: The Effects of Individual Characteristics Upon Academic Performance in the Elementary Grades." *Educational Research Quarterly*, vol. 16, no. 1, 1992.

Kaplan, George. "Shining Lights in High Places: Education's Top Four Leaders and Their Heirs." *Phi Delta Kappan*, September 1985.

———. "The Changing Look of Education's Policy Networks." *Phi Delta Kappan*, May 1992.

Keppel, Francis. "Thank God for the Civil Rights Movement." *Integrated Education*, vol. 3, April/May 1964.

Kohl, Herbert. "Rotten to the Core." *The Nation*, April 6, 1993.

Kozol, Johnathan. "Whittle and the Privateers." *The Nation*, September 21, 1992.

Laird, Susan. "Women and Gender in John Dewey's Philosophy of Education." *Educational Theory*, Winter 1988.

Lerner, Michael. "Jewish New Leftism at Berkeley." *Judaism*, Fall 1969.

McLaughlin, Milbrey Wallin, and Patrick M. Shields. "Involving Low-Income Parents in the Schools: A Role for Policy." *Phi Delta Kappan*, October 1987.

"100 Young Leaders of the Academy." *Change*, October 1978.

Pratte, Richard. "Reconsiderations." *Educational Studies*, Summer 1992.

Ravitch, Diane. "The 'White Flight' Controversy." *The Public Interest*, Spring 1978.

Rederfer, Frederick L. "What Has Happened to Progressive Education?" *The Education Digest*, September 1948.

Reich, Robert B. "Education Reform, Don't Count on Business." *Harper's Magazine*, September 1992.

Reynolds, Gretchen. "The Rising Significance of Race." *Chicago*, December 1992.

Riner, Phillip S. "Dewey's Legacy to Education." *The Educational Forum*, Winter 1989.

Rist, Marilee C. "Business Takes Action in School Reform." *The Education Digest*, November 1990.

———. "Education, Inc." *The American School Board Journal*, September 1991.

———. "Here Comes 'McSchool.'" *The American School Board Journal*, September 1991.

"The School Activists' Library." *The Nation*, September 21, 1992.

Shanker, Albert. "Can Kibbee Lead the Fight for Free Tuition?" *New York Times*, December 2, 1973.

———. "Chelsea Plan Needs Scrutiny." *New York Times*, November 27, 1988.

———. "The Sobol Report." *New York Times*, January 28, 1990.

———. "Multiple Perspectives." *New York Times*, October 27, 1991.

———. "Core Knowledge." *New York Times*, December 16, 1991.

———. "Edison's Candle." *New York Times*, August 29, 1993.

———. "Chelsea Plan Three Years Later." *New York Times*, October 4, 1993.

Shea, William M. "John Dewey and the Crisis of the Canon." *American Journal of Education*, May 1989.

Slavin, Robert E. "IBM's Writing to Read: Is It Right for Reading?" *Phi Delta Kappan*, November 1990.

Timpane, Michael. "Business Has Rediscovered the Public Schools." *Phi Delta Kappan*, February 1984.

Troutman, Benjamin. "A Caution on Cultural Literacy." *Currents* (Washington College), Summer 1988.

Vann, Kimberly R., and Jawanza Kunjufu. "The Importance of an Afrocentric, Multicultural Curriculum." *Phi Delta Kappan*, February 1993.

Wilcox, Preston R. "The Controversy Over I.S. 201." *The Urban Review* (Center for Urban Education), July 1966.

William T. Grant Foundation Commission on Work, Family and Citizenship. "The Forgotten Half: Pathways to Success for America's Youth and Young Families." *Phi Delta Kappan*, December 1988.

Zigler, Edward. "Head Start, The Whole Story." *New York Times*, July 24, 1993, p. 19.

NEWSPAPERS, MAGAZINES, AND NEWSLETTERS

Core Knowledge (promotional literature). Charlottesville, Va.: Core Knowledge Foundation, Summer 1993.

Newsweek. April 19, 1993.

New York Times. October 27, 1939; November 14, 1957; October 30, 1968; January 13, 1974; January 15, 1974; August 31, 1987; April 25, 1990; March 4, 1991; April 26, 1992; February 23, 1993; April 22, 1993; October 5, 1993; October 6, 1993; November 6, 19, 1993; December 14, 1993; December 18, 1993.

The Tablet. December 2, 1939; December 16, 1939.

Virginian Ledger-Star. August 27, 1993; October 14, 1993; October 18, 1993.

INTERVIEWS

Beales, Janet R. Education policy analyst, Reason Foundation, Los Angeles, Calif. October 13, 1993 (telephone).

Connell, Noreen. Executive director, Educational Priorities Panel, New York City. January 5, 1994 (telephone).

Gittell, Marilyn. Director, Howard Samuels Policy Institute, City University of New York, New York City. November 19, 1993 (telephone).

Harris, David O. Professor of history, Old Dominion University. Norfolk, Va., February 4, 1992.

Holley, Ann-Carol Banton. Norfolk, Va., September 28, 1993.

Mooney, Joseph P. Former superintendent of schools, Uniondale, Long Island. Virginia Beach, Va., June 9, 1992.

Nelson, Bob. Public information officer, Colombia University, New York City. December 16, 1993 (telephone).

LETTERS AND MEMORANDA

Berube, Maurice R. Letter to Michael Harrington, chairman, Socialist Party, September 13, 1968.

Hayes, Frederick O. Memorandum to Richard Boone et al. New York City Office of the Mayor, January 21, 1969.

Sobol, Thomas. New York State Commissioner of Education. "Understanding Diversity." Memorandum to New York State Board of Regents, July 12, 1991.

INDEX

About the Author

MAURICE R. BERUBE is Professor of Educational Leadership in the Department of Educational Leadership and Counseling at Old Dominion University. He is the author of *American Presidents and Education* (1991), *Teacher Politics: The Influence of Unions* (1988), and *Education and Poverty: Effective Schooling in the United States and Cuba* (1984), and many more, all published by Greenwood.

Edwards Brothers Inc.
Ann Arbor MI. USA
March 14, 2011